D0275884

THE
ILLUSTRATION
HANDBOOK

THE
ILLUSTRATION
HANDBOOK

A GUIDE TO THE WORLD'S GREATEST ILLUSTRATORS

NICK & TESSA SOUTER

Eagle Editions

AN OCEANA BOOK

Published by
Eagle Editions Ltd
11 Heathfield
Royston
Hertfordshire
SG8 5BW

Copyright©MCMXC
Quarto Publishing Plc

This edition printed 2007

ISBN 978-1-84573-308-7

QUMILHA

This book is produced by
Quantum Publishing Ltd
6 Blundell Street
London N7 9BH

Printed in Singapore by
Star Standard Industries Pte Ltd

Special thanks to
Michael Felmingham, David King,
Mark Hames of Forbidden Planet,
Stuart Newman, Eileen Evans.

FOREWORD

ILLUSTRATION HAS LONG SUFFERED at the hands of even the most well-informed art critic. "Mere illustration" – the most common derogatory remark levelled at paintings that have sought to express or convey an idea – says it all. The cliché is both absurd and meaningless, especially today, when many artists refuse to recognize the artificial barrier between commercial and fine art. Moreover, it does not necessarily follow that an artist working to a brief is little more than a hack. Granted, some are, but the professional illustrator is the modern counterpart of the Renaissance painter, an artist who will frequently transcend the most mundane of briefs to provide the mass audience with Art.

The *Illustrator's Source Book* is a hugely diverse gallery of graphic art created by the world's leading illustrators and proves my case beyond doubt. Here are assembled artists of the book and the magazine, designers of posters, reporters and satirists of the social scene, travellers and painter-illustrators. Popular artists as well as more significant artists, minor figures as well as great ones. In short, the whole spectrum of image-making that comprises the art of illustration. We are first introduced to the illustrators of the 19th century, artists active between 1850 and 1900. Their work appeared in books and magazines aimed at a buoyantly literate middle-class public, to whom reading had become as much a habit as watching television is to us today. For almost an entire century these artists were at the mercy of the engraver. Until the late 1870s, Victorian printing technology was compelled to rely on wood-engraving as the sole means of reproducing an artist's design. It was a laborious process which usually obliterated the spontaneity of an original, although occasionally it could produce surprises. Only if the artist was familiar with the practice of drawing *directly* onto the woodblock with brush or pen and black ink could idiosyncrasies of style survive. Adolf Von Menzel in Germany, Charles Keene and Houghton in Britain, were foremost among those who learnt from Hokusai and other masters of the *Ukiyo-e*. Guided by enlightened master engravers like the Brothers Dalziel, Joseph Swain and William Luson Thomas, they succeeded in overcoming the daunting limitations of the medium.

As the 19th century drew to an end, photomechanical technology came to the rescue, making possible a breakthrough in both colour printing and in reproduction of black-and-white originals. This was the decade of Aubrey Beardsley and Phil May, of Charles Dana Gibson and Howard Pyle, of EJ Sullivan and Paul Renouard. At this time also, the painter's contribution to illustration grew rapidly, now that it had become possible to reproduce drawings with great fidelity. One of the pleasures of looking through Parisian weeklies of the era, such as *L'Assiette au Beurre* and *Le Rire,* is in discovering editorial drawings by Juan Gris, Eugène Higgins, Frantisek Kupka, Lautrec, Jacques Villon and Kees Van Dongen, not forgetting the dramatic input of Kathe Kollwitz, Alfred Kubin and Jules Pascin in the pages of the Munich weekly, *Simplicissimus.*

Good illustration, of course, knows no frontiers. If at one period the ball is not to be found in the court of the British or the Americans, it will be found in the court of the French or the Germans. One thinks of the revival of lithography which led to the golden era of the poster in *belle époque* France. One thinks also of the Berlin of the 1920s and of the extraordinary satirical journalism in which a brilliant generation of editors, poets and essayists made common cause with artists like George Grosz, Otto Dix and John Heartfield, to castigate what they felt to be an unjust system.

Indeed, the ball goes back and forth constantly. One is also reminded of American illustration of this time; the advent of superb story illustration in the *Saturday Evening Post* and *Collier's,* a reportorial tradition which lasted through World War II and into the 1960s in *Fortune, Sports Illustrated and Rolling Stone.* In fact, American illustration flourishes right up to the present day in a host of new periodicals which also publish a younger generation of European illustrators, thus ensuring the cross-fertilization that is such a vital part of illustration.

William Morris maintained that illustration, though not vital to people's existence, nonetheless gave a great deal of aesthetic pleasure and was therefore a subject worthy of attention and encouragement. The *Illustrator's Source Book* confirms this to be true in no uncertain terms.

Paul Hogarth

INTRODUCTION

BEFORE ASSESSING THE ROLE of the illustrator within society it is perhaps appropriate to consider first his or her position in the world of art.

For many years the notion has prevailed that, in the company of fine artists, the illustrator is something of a second-class citizen. This discrimination is predicated on the belief that the painter or sculptor is an unfettered spirit whose work gives free reign to self expression and whose art makes statements of an intensely personal nature. Illustrators, on the other hand, are the slaves of commerce – they are invariably commissioned to produce their work, and their inspiration derives, not from personal experience, but from the source material with which they are provided.

Under scrutiny, this delineation quickly blurs. Some of the world's greatest art treasures were in fact commissioned, whether by the Church, the State or by private individuals. For example, Michelangelo's paintings in the Sistine Chapel, while infused with an intensely personal vision, were nonetheless inspired by the writings of that all-time best seller, the Bible.

The fact is that all artists, whether painters, sculptors or illustrators, face very much the same predicament: they all work within constraints from which only the power of their imagination can free them. With the skills and materials available to them, they endeavour to create a unique interpretation of an idea, event or observation, and it is this shared aim that validates the role of illustrator within the world of the arts.

Historically, there have been differing schools of thought on the role of illustration. At one extreme we have Eric Gill, who believed that illustration should "really illustrate, clarify and illuminate the text" and not be used for "outpourings of sensibility". At the other extreme, we find the German Expressionist illustrators, such as Lovis Corinth, whose drawings were seldom literal and who often subordinated the illustration of the text to the expression of the artist's state of mind. And quite outside of this spectrum there was the Edwardian passion for gift books, which merely served as vehicles for the artists' explorations of their illustrative, imaginative and decorative skills. However, irrespective of the style adopted and the subject matter chosen, the illustrator performs simultaneously, and sometimes unwittingly, in a secondary role – that of social historian.

Our view of history would be somewhat myopic were it not illuminated by such a wealth of illustrations for both fictional and documentary material. In Britain, artists such as John Everett Millais and Fred Walker meticulously recorded the details of Victorian life in illustrations for contemporary novels by Trollope and Thackeray. Less inadvertent were the commentaries on the state of the nation by Frank Holl and Luke Fildes, who set out to expose the poverty of urban life, or the scathing satires of monarchy, society and politics by Gillray, Rowlandson and Cruickshank. Even the 1890s passion for nostalgic and idealized depictions of country life informs us of a yearning for a pre-industrial world. In fact there is very little in the way of human behaviour and feeling that has escaped the conscious investigation or unconscious recording of the illustrator.

Another role, now mostly usurped by the camera, is that of the illustrator as journalist. With the development of the newspaper in the middle of the 18th century there was an increasing demand for the pictorial coverage of topical events. In 1854 William Simpson was sent on assignment to the Crimea, and his drawings of the war mark the arrival of the "Special Artist", now more simply known as War Artist. The conditions and dangers of battle, combined with the urgency of the public's demand for the very latest information, meant that artists rarely had time to do more than sketch the situation, despatch the drawing and rely on the finishing artists at home to add the details. Yet, despite the aesthetic compromises that such disconnected teamwork entailed, the artist could still capture the spirit of the occasion.

Today, in matters of reportage, the camera reigns supreme over illustration for a public which prefers to construct its own interpretation of events seen, with apparent objectivity, through the eye of a lens. However, the tradition of the artist as reporter continues, and in many countries the courtroom remains an arena of human interest to which only the illustrator, and not the photographer, has access.

Of course, the involvement of the artist in current affairs is not limited to crime and war. A sphere of influence which remains as strong today as it ever did is caricature. While politicians and royalty may shield their eyes from the flash guns of the *paparazzi* there is no escaping this cruelly exaggerated, yet precise, form of cartoon drawing. The word caricature is derived from the Italian *caricare*, which means "to overload", and it was in Italy during the mid to late 1500s that the artist Annibale Carracci discovered that if he deliberately overemphasized the characteristics of his friends he could "grasp the perfect deformity and thus reveal the very essence of a personality". During the 18th century this art form became popular with dilettantes and amateurs who had embarked upon the Grand Tour. But by the 1900s, when there was a fascination with the belief that physiognomy revealed a near-scientific insight into personality, caricature had fallen into the hands of serious political artists, who used it to pass judgement on topical events and lampoon the conceits of public figures.

There are few newspapers now in circulation that do not employ the talents of a caricaturist or political cartoonist. Depending on the editorial stance of the publication, these skills may be used simply to amuse the reader, or to seriously ridicule and possibly damage the credibility of the individuals depicted. It is this latter faculty that leads us to consider yet another role of the illustrator – that of propagandist.

Part of the psychosis of war involves the dehumanization of the opposing forces and, to this end the art of the caricaturist can be used to supreme jingoistic effect. Since the development of newspapers and posters, there has not been a war effort or revolution that has not recruited ranks of illustrators to portray the enemy or oppressor as a gargoyle of iniquity. Some of the finest examples are to be found in the works of David Moor and Viktor Deni from the time of the Russian Revolution. Their vilification of the bourgeoisie as bloated, pig-like creatures could not have failed to focus the rage of the proletariat by reducing complex issues to simple, powerful symbols.

Although most extreme in times of conflict, the manipulative power of the illustrator has its place in peacetime, where it is used to great effect in the world of commerce and advertising. The same talents and techniques that can so successfully defame, can be just as effective in the process of idealization.

Advertising agencies did not start to appear in any great number until the 1920s, but the business itself dates back to the middle of the 19th century when, for the most part, it was in the hands of the manufacturers. For the first 50 years, in the absence of photography, the principal role of the artist was simply to draw an image of the product. But as competition increased it became necessary to create perceived differentials in virtually identical products, so as to legitimize superiority claims. This sleight of hand was accomplished by the illustrator, who created an image world into which the client's product could be placed in the most flattering light. A particularly good example is the sale in the late 1890s of Millais' painting *Bubbles* to the manufacturers of Pears' Soap. In its original form this sentimental depiction of a child blowing bubbles with soap suds would have evoked gentle feelings of innocence, the freshness of youth, beauty, protectiveness and warmth. With the addition of the Pears' logo at the top of the image, and a bar of Pears' soap near the feet of the child, many of these emotions would have been grafted onto the product, which could then be presented to the public as a safe, pure and wholesome way of cleansing the skin. Millais himself is said to have been outraged, but the campaign was enormously successful and nearly 100 years later it is possible to trace the imagery of Pears' advertising back to Millais' work.

As well as creating a suitable emotional and aesthetic context for a product, illustration also developed many of advertising's most effective selling tools – visual hyperboles for the exaggeration of quality, the animation of company logos for branding, the exploitation of the female form and, perhaps most important, the use of humour. The public may get tired of advertising but it never gets tired of laughing.

And humour, exemplified by John Gilroy's cartoon advertisements for Guinness in the 1930s and 40s, can engage the attention and sympathy of even the most disaffected audience.

That humour should reach advertising via the illustrator is hardly surprising, since the role of entertainer is traditional to the artist. The cartoon strip, first developed by the German artist Wilhelm Busch in the mid-19th century, is now a feature of daily life—and since the early 1840s there has been a proliferation of magazines whose primary concern is to amuse.

Humour, however, plays little part in the last role that we should consider here, that of illustrator as teacher. This category needs to be broad enough to include the topographical work of such artists as A B Houghton, who visited the United States in 1870 and whose drawings helped to satisfy the craving for travel literature at that time. But it must also embrace the meticulous work of those technical illustrators who make the worlds of science, technology and nature comprehensible to us. Their skills face increasing competition from photography, which, along with complex computer graphics and digital technology, can now offer an illustrator's control over images that originated inside a camera. For some that challenge will once again raise the illustrator-as-artist debate with the contention that the technical illustrator is no more than a copyist whose interpretive skills are put to little use. Be that as it may, the acknowledgement of those skills is important here, as without them we would have an incomplete picture of the multifarious roles that illustration plays in our world.

In putting together this book we have tried to cover the major twists and turns in illustration's developmental path since the middle of the 19th century. We have found that for much of this journey, illustrators have paid little heed to the direction of fine art and their progress cannot be described by a series of "isms" and schools of thought. However, many figures, such as Morris, Abbey, Pyle and Gill have exerted a lasting influence on the course that illustration is taking and we have tried to ensure that they are well represented.

Inevitably, due to the limitations of space and the scarcity of good material for reproduction, there are omissions and you may find that a favourite artist has not been included. For this we apologize, while hoping that, as a source book of styles, you will still find this volume to be comprehensive and inspiring.

Our lasting impression as we come to the end of compiling these images is that at every point in its history illustration has been on the threshold of an exciting new development – and never more so than today. Technology and imagination, it would seem, know no bounds, and when one considers that illustrators can now generate original artwork on a Mackintosh computer, one can only wonder as to what the future may bring.

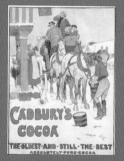

CHAPTER
ONE

BY 1850 THE STAGE WAS SET for the dramatic entrance of the illustrator as the entertainer of the 19th century. In reaction to the bleakness of the Napoleonic war period, the previous years had seen a craving for culture spread across Europe. Literacy was increasing, and with the Victorian invention of the armchair and sofa, the first truly comfortable items of furniture, a new concept in urban recreation evolved: family get-togethers with reading material of one form or another providing the amusement.

At the same time the Industrial Revolution also provided the technology for mass marketing, and with the arrival of metal printing plates and chromolithography, publishers were in a position to satisfy the public's thirst for entertainment and knowledge. Their industry was transformed beyond recognition.

In mid-century France the relaxing of censorship laws, coupled with the artistic freedom afforded by the autographic litho process, encouraged a flourishing tradition of caricature. Surprisingly, in Britain it had the opposite effect: caricaturists who had achieved prominence in such magazines as *Punch* found that the litho stone softened their work, which then lacked the spiteful line more easily achieved on copper plate.

During these years London artistic life exerted a huge influence throughout the world of illustrators. The political upheavals on the Continent had led many disaffected artists to Britain, and their influence was in part responsible for the development of social realism between 1850 and 1890. The illustrations of the lives of the poor by artists such as Luke Fildes and Frank Holl were then exported to the world at large through the distribution of such magazines as *The Graphic* and *The Illustrated London News*, which were eagerly read by artists in America and on the Continent.

As this frenzy of illustrative activity continued, various schools of thought began to emerge from the community of artists and critics. In 1848 John Everett Millais, William Holman Hunt and Dante Gabriel Rossetti formed the Pre-Raphaelite Brotherhood in an attempt to recreate the naivety and moral realism of early Renaissance painting.

With their strong literary leanings they are accredited by many with giving illustration the status of art and encouraging the practice of putting artists' names on the covers of books.

The 1860s are sometimes described as the "golden age of Victorian illustration". There was a fashion for drawings of contemporary life in the novels of Dickens, Thackeray and Trollope, newsagents and bookstalls were appearing in every street and at every railway station, libraries were making their first appearance and taxes had been repealed on newspapers, making them more affordable. During this period specialist magazines were developed, and in 1860 *The Queen,* the first magazine aimed directly at women, appeared and was such a success that other publishers soon followed suit. Magazines were enjoying similar popularity on the other side of the Atlantic where, with the development of half-tone reproduction, the American public was eagerly reading *Harper's, Century* and *McClure's* and enjoying the work of Charles Marion Russell and Howard Pyle.

After a brief period of decline in the 1870s, the 1880s saw a resurgence of interest and activity in book production. This was due in part to the influence of William Morris, the leading figure in the Arts and Crafts Movement as well as the private press movement, which had an impact on both European and American publishing. Morris founded the Kelmscott Press in 1891 and, with his principal illustrator Edward Burne-Jones, revived the tradition of medieval craftsmanship and the art of the woodcut and helped create what he referred to as the age of the "Book Beautiful".

The intensely art-conscious 1890s saw the emergence of the Aesthetic Movement, which followed the ethos of "art for art's sake" and which Morris despised. Its style of *fin de siècle* morbidity and eroticism was best captured by Aubrey Beardsley, whose drawings were particularly suited to the process reproduction of the day. The Aesthetes were championed by Oscar Wilde, and although his eventual disgrace brought the movement into disrepute, the contribution of such exponents as Walter Crane, Randolph Caldecott and Kate Greenaway was critical to the subsequent development of fantasy illustration.

But the new processes did not just revolutionize book production. In the hands of Jules Cheret (who pioneered many of the developments in chromolithographic poster printing), Toulouse-Lautrec and Alphonse Mucha, they led to another golden age, that of the poster. This medium, which was to become so important to the advertising industry in the next century, became one of the most popular art forms, with members of the public literally tearing posters from the hoardings and taking them home.

CHAPTER ONE

*Born in Philadelphia, USA.
Worked in a wood engraving
studio and studied art
at evening classes at the
Pennsylvania Academy of Fine
Arts. In 1871 he moved to New
York, where the influence of
French and German black and
white art was transforming pen
drawing. He produced small
black and white illustrations
for Harpers and Brothers, then
illustrated some of their more
successful books, including*
Christmas Stories *by Charles
Dickens (1875),* Selections from
the Poetry of Robert Herrick
(1882) and Oliver Goldsmith's
She Stoops to Conquer *(1887).
In 1878 he settled in England
and became a prolific illustrator,
specialising in costume and
figure subjects. In contrast to
the decorative convention of the
period his meticulous attention
to detail – which extended to his
making every effort to achieve
historical accuracy – achieved a
realism that influenced a whole
generation of younger artists. He
exhibited his first oil painting at
the Royal Academy in 1890, and
was elected Royal Academician
in 1902.*

1, 2 *BOOK:* SHE STOOPS TO
CONQUER *by Oliver Goldsmith*
DATE: c. 1887

3, 4 *BOOK:* SCHOOL FOR
SCANDAL *by Richard Sheridan*
DATE: 1885

1

2

3

4

Apparently untrained, he contributed to The Comic Times *and* Comic News *between 1855 and 1865, when he joined* Punch *magazine. He illustrated several books, including Bunyan's* Pilgrim's Progress *(1859),* Nine Lives of a Cat *(1860),* Stories Little Breeches Told *(1862) and* The Fables of Aesop *(1857). He also illustrated for a number of magazines, including* The Illustrated Times, The Cornhill Magazine, Every Boy's Magazine *and* Punch.

1- 3 *BOOK:* THE FABLES OF AESOP
DATE: 1857

1

2

3

1

2

3

SIR EDWARD COLEY BURNE-JONES (1833-1898)

Born in Birmingham, UK. He was educated at Oxford University, where he met William Morris, with whom he toured Belgium and the cathedrals of northern France instead of completing his studies. On his return to England he worked with Dante Gabriel Rossetti on the Morte D'Arthur murals at the Oxford Union in 1857-8 and was on the fringes of the Pre-Raphaelite Brotherhood. Known foremost as a painter, he also illustrated a number of books, including Archibald Maclarens The Fairy Family *(1857), Morris's* The Earthly Paradise, *which was never completed,* The Works of Geoffrey Chaucer *(1896) and Dalziel's* Bible Gallery *(1881). Between 1892 and 1898 he designed books for the Kelmscott Press. He received an honorary degree from Oxford in 1881, was made a baronet in 1894 and in 1889 won the Cross of the Legion of Honour at the Paris Exposition.*

1 *BOOK:* GOOD WORDS
DATE: 1862

2 *BOOK:* BIBLE GALLERY *by Dalziel*
DATE: 1881

3 *PAINTING:* "THE DEPTHS OF THE SEA"
DATE: 1886

WALTER CRANE
(1845-1915)

Born in Liverpool UK. His illustrating career began in 1863, when he was commissioned by Edmund Evans to illustrate three toy books for Warne publishers. Other books he illustrated include The House That Jack Built *(1865),* The Baby's Opera *(1877),* The Baby's Bouquet *(1878), Edmund Spenser's* The Faerie Queene *(published in 19 parts, 1894-97),* Ali Baba and the Forty Thieves *(1873) and* The Happy Prince and Other Stories *by Oscar Wilde (1888). Crane was also a painter, writer and designer of textiles, wallpapers and ceramics. His work was characterized by strong outlines, flat tints and solid blacks, and was influenced by his study of early printed books, medieval illuminations, Japanese prints and the work of the Pre-Raphaelites. He was converted to "conscious" socialism by William Morris and became a primary figure in the Arts and Crafts movement. In 1883 he joined the Socialist League and in 1884 was the first president of the Art Workers' Guild. He taught design at Manchester School of Art, was Art Director at Reading College and Principal of the Royal College of Art, 1898-99.*

1, 4 *BOOK:* THE BLUEBEARD
PICTURE BOOK
DATE: 1899

2 *BOOK:* ARTHURIAN LEGENDS
DATE: NOT KNOWN

3 *BOOK:* A FLOWER WEDDING
DATE: NOT KNOWN

5 *BOOK:* A ROMANCE OF THE
THREE Rs
DATE: 1886

6 *BOOK:* THE BABY'S BOUQUET
DATE: 1878

1

2

3

But said, that in the future years the Princess young should die, | In vain in all her father's Court the spinning-wheel's forbid | And down she falls in death-like sleep : they lay her on her bed,
By pricking of a spindle-point—ah, woeful prophecy! | In vain in all the country-side the spindles sharp are hid; | And all around her sink to rest—a palace of the dead!
But now, a kind young Fairy, who had waited to the last, [are past; | For in a lonely turret high, and up a winding stair, [care. | A hundred years pass—still they sleep, and all around the place
Stepped forth, and said, "No, she shall sleep till a hundred years | There lives an ancient woman who still turns her wheel with | A wood of thorns has risen up—no path a man can trace.
"And then she shall be wakened by a King's son—truth I tell— | The Princess found her out one day, and tried to learn to spin; | At last, a King's son, in the hunt, asked how long it had stood;
"And he will take her for his wife, and all will yet be well." | Alas! the spindle pricked her hand—the charm had entered in! | And what old towers were those he saw above the ancient wood.

4

5

6

WILHELM BUSC
(1832-1908)

Born in Hanover, Germany. Studied at academies in Dusseldorf, Antwerp and Munich. In 1859, his drawings began to appear in the leading comic weekly Fliegende Blatter, *but he soon moved from work for periodicals to self-contained albums of comic-strip narratives with verses accompanying the images. In this way he was able to develop the comic-strip form more fully and his work included social satire and cautionary tales. His best-known characters were the naughty children Max and Moritz, whose wicked pranks gave rein to Busch's talent for slapstick humour, but he was an innovative artist, producing graphic equivalents for emotional reactions and physical movement which subsequently became conventions of comic-strip art.*

1.2 *BOOK:* BUZZ ABUZZ
DATE: 1872

3 *BOOK:* MAX UNDMORITZ
DATE: 1871

1

2

3

1

*Born in Kent, UK. He was
educated at William Dadson's
Academy of Art and the Royal
Academy Schools in London,
where he won the medal
for life drawing in 1840. He
contributed illustrations for* The
Book of British Ballads *(1842)
and illustrated the frontispiece
for* The Kentish Coronal *(1840).
Dadd went insane while on a
European tour with Sir Thomas
Phillips and was eventually
committed to a mental asylum
after he murdered his father in
1843. While in the asylum he
was encouraged to continue
painting and produced works of
incredible delicacy and beauty.*

1 *PAINTING:* THE FAIRY
FELLER'S MASTER STROKE
DATE: 1864

RICHARD DOYLE
(1824-1883)

Born in London. He started drawing from a very early age and produced his first book Home for the Holidays *(published in 1887), when he was only 12. His first published work, the comic medieval book* The Eglinton Tournament *(1840), was a great success. From 1843 he contributed regularly to* Punch, *and in January 1844 designed its sixth cover, a procession of figures based on Titian's "Bacchus and Ariadne" which remained unchanged until 1954. He eventually resigned from the magazine in protest against its anti-Catholic views and for the rest of his career concentrated on illustrating books. His own* Manners and Customs of Ye Englishe *(1849) and* Bird's Eye Views of Society *(1864) made him a household name. He also illustrated* The Fairy Ring *by the Brothers Grimm (1845), Mark Lemon's* The Enchanted Doll *(1849), Ruskin's* The King of the Golden River *(1851) and, his masterpiece, William Allingham's* In Fairyland *(1870), the illustrations for which were put to a new story in 1884,* The Princess Nobody *by Andrew Lang.*

1 *PAINTING:* "THE KNIGHT AND THE SPECTRE"
DATE: NOT KNOWN

2 *BOOK:* THE PRINCESS NOBODY *by A D Lang*
DATE: 1884

3, 4 *BOOK:* IN FAIRYLAND *by William Allingham*
DATE: 1870

1

2

3

4

Born in Liverpool UK. Studied at Warrington School of Art and the South Kensington and Royal Academy Schools in London. He was renowned as a black and white artist in the social realist vein, producing powerful images of the poor and the destitute. Fildes' drawing of Charles Dickens' study, entitled "The Empty Chair", done the day after the author's death, was published in The Graphic *and was the inspiration for van Gogh's painting "The Yellow Chair". Fildes' illustrations also appeared in* Sunday Magazine, The Cornhill Magazine *and* The Gentleman's Magazine. *He illustrated a number of books, including Thackeray's* Catherine *(1894) and Dickens'* Edwin Drood *(1869). He decided to concentrate on painting after 1872 and became a major portrait painter of the Edwardian era. He was elected to the Royal Academy in 1887 and was knighted in 1906.*

1 *MAGAZINE:* SUNDAY MAGAZINE *DATE: 1866*

2 *MAGAZINE:* SUNDAY MAGAZINE *DATE: 1868*

3 *MAGAZINE:* SUNDAY MAGAZINE *DATE: 1868*

2

3

1

2

3

*Born in London. He entered the
Government School of Design at
Somerset House at the unusually
young age of 14, and at 15
enrolled at the Royal Academy
Schools, where he won the silver
medal for antique drawing
two years later. In 1851 he first
came into contact with the
Pre-Raphaelite Brotherhood
and was subsequently involved
in the painting of the Oxford
Union murals with Dante
Gabriel Rossetti and others.
He also painted a number of
famous pictures, including*
"Home from the Sea" *and* "The
Long Engagement". *Hughes
is best known for his black
and white work and for his
insistence on integrating his
illustrations into the design of
the book as a whole. His most
notable period as an illustrator
was his association with the
writer George MacDonald on
books such as* At the Back of
the North Wind *(1871),* The
Princess and the Goblin *(1872)
and* Phantasies *(1905). He also
illustrated for magazines such
as* The Graphic *and* Good Words
for the Young.

1 *PAINTING:* "ALICE IN
WONDERLAND"
DATE: NOT KNOWN

2,3 *MAGAZINE:* GOOD WORDS
FOR THE YOUNG
DATE: 1871

PAUL GUSTAVE CHRISTOPHE
DORE (1832-1883)

*Born in Strasbourg. He learned
lithography while still at school
in Bourg-en-Bresse. At the age
of 11 his family moved to Paris,
where eventually he was placed
under contract to Charles
Philippon's* Journal Pour Rire,
*contributing a weekly page.
He had his first lithographs
published at the age of 13 and
by the age of 22 he was already
famous for his illustrated*
Rabelais. *There followed a
series of classic titles, including
Dante's* Divine Comedy *(1861),
Coleridge's* Rime of the Ancient
Mariner *(1865), Tennyson's*
The Story of King Arthur and
Queen Guinevere *(1868)
and Milton's* Paradise Lost
*(1866). He also produced his
own book of caricatures,* Two
Hundred Sketches, Humorous
and Grotesque *(1867). His
work appeared in many
publications, including* The
Illustrated London News *and*
The Illustrated Times.

1-4 *BOOK:* VISION OF HELL
by Dante
DATE.1860

5 *BOOK:* GARGANTUAET
PANTAGRUEL *by François
Rabelais*
DATE: NOT KNOWN

1

2

3

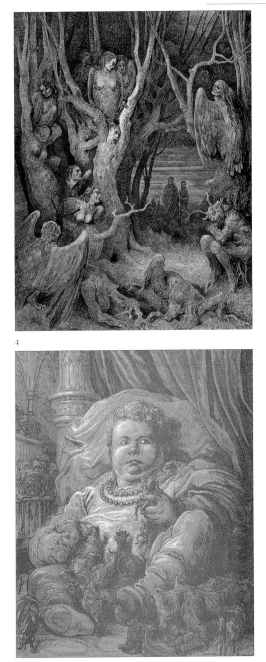

4

5

Born in London. Studied
medicine at St Bartholomew's
Hospital before deciding to
become an artist. He soon
made his name as a black and
white artist, and illustrated
for a number of periodicals,
including The Sporting Review,
Illustrated London Magazine,
New Monthly Magazine and
The London Magazine. In 1840
he joined the staff of Bentley's
Miscellany, and in 1841 he
found a platform for his own
brand of pictorial satire in
the newly established journal
Punch. But he was best known
for his caricatures depicting
Victorian middle-class life,
epitomized in the characters
of Tom Noddy and Mr Briggs.
Books illustrated include
Etchings and Sketchings (1835),
The Ingoldsby Legends (1840),
Jack the Giant Killer (1843) and
Uncle Tom's Cabin (1852).

1 BOOK: ASK MAMMA by R S
Surtees
DATE. 1858

2 MAGAZINE: PUNCH
DATE. 1881

1

2

"BUBBLES."
By Sir JOHN MILLAIS, Bt., P.R.A.
After the Original in the possession of Messrs. PEARS

1

*Born in Southampton, UK.
Studied at the Royal Academy
Schools. In 1848 he founded
the Pre-Raphaelite Brotherhood
with Dante Gabriel Rossetti and
Holman Hunt. He was much
admired for his brilliant black-
and-white illustrations, which,
like those of the American
Edwin Austin Abbey, show an
incredible attention to detail
and a concern for realism,
both visual and moral. He
illustrated the novels of Anthony
Trollope, which were serialised
in* The Cornhill Magazine
in 1860, and contributed to
Punch *and the Pre-Raphaelite
magazine* The Germ. *His best
period is considered to have
ended by 1863, when he was
elected Royal Academician, by
which time he had given up
illustrating in favour of painting
portraits and landscapes. In
1885 he was made a baronet
and in 1896 became President
of the Royal Academy, which he
remained until his death from
throat cancer six months later.*

1 *ADVERTISEMENT:* PEARS
SOAP *(based on the original
painting, "Bubbles")*
DATE: 1896

2, 3 *BOOK:* THE DALZIEL
BIBLE
DATE: 1864

2

3

*English but born in Paris,
the son of a frustrated opera
singer. He moved to London
as a child and showed an
early talent for drawing. In
1851 he studied chemistry at
University College, London,
but left in 1856 to study art
in Paris, where he met James
McNeill Whistler and E J
Poynter. From 1857 to 1860
he studied in Antwerp under
De Keyser and Van Lerius, but
the loss of an eye forced him to
abandon his plans to become
a painter and he returned to
London to pursue a career as
a black and white artist. From
1860 he became a regular
contributor to Punch with his
caricatures poking fun at the
Victorian bourgeoisie. He was
the greatest social satirist of
the period and the accuracy of
his ink drawings provides a
complete chronicle of Victorian
life.* He also illustrated for
Harpers, The Graphic, The
Illustrated Times *and* The
Cornhill *magazine, and in
middle age he wrote and
illustrated three novels,* Peter
Ibbetson *(1891),* Trilby *(1894)*
and The Martian *(1896).*

1

2

1 *BOOK:* TRILBY *by George Du
Maurier
DATE.* 1894

2 *BOOK:* OUR LIFE
DATE: 1865

3 *MAGAZINE:* CORNHILL
MAGAZINE
DATE: 1863

4 *BOOK:* GOOD WORDS
DATE. 1861

5 *BOOK:* PICTURES OF
ENGLISH LITERATURE
DATE: 1870

6 *MAGAZINE:* PUNCH
DATE: c. 1860

3

4

5

6

EDWARD LEAR
(1812-1888)

Born in London. His unmarried sister Ann taught him to paint and, by the age of 15, he was already setting his drawings of birds. He made his name with his superb hand-coloured illustrations of parrots, published in 1832 as The Family of Psittacidae, or Parrots. From 1832-36 Lear was employed by the Earl of Derby to draw his collection of rare birds and animals for a book, the privately printed Knowsley Menagerie (1856). For the amusement of the earl's children, he composed and illustrated humorous limericks in a deliberately childish, but wonderfully expressive style. These were published in 1846 as A Book of Nonsense, the popularity of which remained confined to upper-class households until a revised version of the book published by Routledge-Warne in 1861, became a best-seller. His most famous rhymes, Hey Diddle Diddle and The Owl and the Pussycat, from Nonsense Songs, Stories, Botany and Alphabets (1871), are perennial favourites, probably more popular today than ever. His last book Laughable Lyrics, was published in 1871.

1, 2 BOOK: THE LEAR ALPHABET by Edward Lear
DATE: 1871

3, 4 BOOK: A BOOK OF NONSENSE by Edward Lear
DATE: 1846

1

2

There was an Old Man of Marseilles, whose daughters wore bottle-green veils:
They caught several Fish, which they put in a dish,
And sent to their Pa at Marseilles.

3

There was an Old Man of Corfu, who never knew what he should do;
So he rushed up and down, till the sun made him brown,
That bewildered Old Man of Corfu.

4

1

Born in Philadelphia, USA. At the age of 23 his first illustrated book, Out of the Hurly Burly, *sold over a million copies and launched his career. Frost was loved by Americans for his warm and humorous portrayal of animals and people. He was a master draughtsman and his drawings captured the mood and detail of rural American life. He had a remarkable sense of colour values, yet he was colour blind and his wife or sons had to label the colours of his palette for him. He illustrated the novels of Mark Twain, in which he created the enduring images of Tom Sawyer and Huckleberry Finn, but he is best known for his illustrations for Joel Chandler Harris's* Uncle Remus *and* Brer Rabbit *stories. In 1876 he joined the staff of* Harper's *and was cartoonist on the* New York Daily Graphic *for 20 years.*

1, 2 *BOOK:* UNCLE REMUS *by J Chandler Harris*
DATE: 1893

3, 4 *BOOK; A TANGLED TALE by Lewis Carroll*
DATE: 1886

2

3

4

*Born in Kotagiri Madras.
Educated in England at Leigh'
s Academy and the Royal
Academy Schools, where he
came under the influence of
the Pre-Raphaelite Brotherhood
and developed an interest in
Japanese prints — the effects of
which are particularly evident
in his illustrations for Dalziel's*
Arabian Nights *(1864). In 1869*
The Graphic *magazine sent him
on a journalistic assignment to
the USA to draw the Americans
and their way of life. The results
are among his best work.
His illustrated books include*
Longfellow's Poems *(1867) and
Dalziel's* Bible Gallery *(1880),
and he contributed to* The
Argosy, Every Boy's Magazine,
The Sunday Magazine, The
Graphic *and* The Broadway.

1, 2 *BOOK:* ARABIAN NIGHTS
DATE: 1864

3 *MAGAZINE:* THE SUNDAY
MAGAZINE
DATE: 1867

4 *MAGAZINE:* THE SUNDAY
MAGAZINE
DATE: 1867

1

2

3   4

1

2

*Born in London. In spite of
being accidentally blinded
in one eye during a fencing
match with his father, he was a
superb draughtsman and was
essentially self-taught, having
studied only briefly at the Royal
Academy Schools and the
Clipstone Street Life Academy.
His illustrations to Aesop's
Fables (1848) brought him to the
attention of Punch magazine,
then at its most radical. He
replaced Doyle as a full-time
member of staff in 1851, and his
pencil drawings over the next 50
years summed up the essence of
Victorian society. He illustrated
a number of books, but is best
known for his illustrations to the
first edition of Lewis Carroll's
Alice in Wonderland (1865).
This was a difficult commission
because Carroll, disappointed
at having his own illustrations
for the book rejected by the
publisher, consequently wanted
complete artistic control over
Tenniel which led to a great
many arguments. Because of
these difficulties, and in spite of
the fact that Alice in Wonderland
achieved international acclaim
on publication, Tenniel initially
refused to illustrate the
subsequent Alice Through the
Looking Glass. He finally gave
in, however, and it came out in
1871, when it was an instant
success. He was knighted in
1893 and retired from Punch
magazine at the age of 80.*

1 *MAGAZINE:* PUNCH
DATE: 1853

2 *MAGAZINE:* PUNCH
DATE: 1853

3 *BOOK:* ALICE THROUGH
THE LOOKING GLASS *by Lewis
Carroll*
DATE: 1871

3

Born in Slough, UK. Studied animal anatomy at the South Kensington School of Art, and animal painting under Frank W Calderon. Aldin's activities as a huntsman enabled him to draw the funny side of English country life, and his comic hunting scenes, olde worlde inns and dog-portraits, drawn in a jovial style, were immensely popular. He was particularly well known for his series of Puppy Dog *books (1904—14), which were favourites with children.* Books include Hodder and Stoughton's Christmas Eve *(1910), which owes much to the influence of Caldecott, and Anna Sewell's* Black Beauty *(1912).* He contributed to numerous periodicals during the 1890s, including The English Illustrated Magazine, Lady's Pictorial, Boy's Own Paper *and* Illustrated Sporting and Dramatic News.

1 *ADVERTISEMENT:* COLMAN'S
BLUE
DATE: 1898

2 *ADVERTISEMENT:* COLMAN'S
STARCH
DATE: c. 1898

3 *ADVERTISEMENT:* CADBURY'S
COCOA
DATE. c. 1899

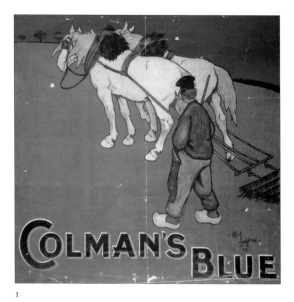

1

2

3

1

2

*Born in Staffordshire, UK.
Studied art in London and
Paris, where meeting with
Grasset proved a strong
influence towards a career
in poster design. He then
emigrated to the USA, where
he settled in Brooklyn. His
work included portraits,
posters and lithographs,
ceramics, watercolour and line
illustrations. Clients included
The New York Sun, Scribner's
and The Century. Rheads style
owed much to Art Nouveau,
but he was criticized for weak
drawing, sometimes masked by
over-elaboration of decorative
elements. He collaborated
with his brothers George and
Frederick, individually and as
a team, on book illustrations
– The Pilgrim's Progress (1898),
Tennyson's Idylls of the King
(1898) and Robinson Crusoe
(1900). He illustrated children's
stories for Harper's Bazaar, and
his own book as author and
illustrator, Bold Robin Hood and
his Outlaw Band, was published
in 1923.*

3

4

1 *ADVERTISEMENT:* THE SUN
MAGAZINE
DATE: 1894

2 *MAGAZINE COVER:* THE
CENTURY
DATE. c. 1895

3 *MAGAZINE COVER:*
SCRIBNER'S
DATE: c. 1895

4 *ADVERTISEMENT:*
LUNDBORG PERFUME
DATE. c. 1895

THE LADY OF THE LAKE
TELLETH ARTHVR OF THE
SWORD EXCALIBVR

1

2

4   5

Born in Brighton, UK. His family circumstances precluded any formal art training, though he had shown a talent for drawing and caricature while at school. While he was working as a clerk in London the artist Edward Burne-Jones encouraged him to attend evening classes at Westminster School of Art. In 1892 he visited Paris, where he was inspired by the posters of Toulouse-Lautrec and the current interest in Japanese prints. His first commission was from Messrs Dent, who asked him to illustrate their new edition of Malory's Le Morte d'Arthur (1893). He then became Art Editor of The Yellow Book quarterly (1894-96) and illustrator for The Savoy (1896-98). Books illustrated include Pope's The Rape of the Lock (1896), The Lysistrata of Aristophanes (1896), Oscar Wilde's Salomé (1894) and A Book of Fifty Drawings by Aubrey Beardsley (189 7). He developed his own highly personal version of the Art Nouveau style, featuring highly stylized forms, sinuous curves and the use of areas of heavy decoration set against areas of white space. His fascination with the decadence of the fin-de-siècle period was reflected in the sinister eroticism of his images, which shocked the public at the time. The acknowledged genius of black and white art, he influenced many subsequent artists. He died of tuberculosis at 25.

1 BOOK: LE MORTE D'ARTHUR
by Malory
DATE: 1893

2, 3 MAGAZINE COVER: THE
SAVOY
DATE: 1896

4,5 BOOK: SALOME
by Oscar Wilde
DATE: 1894

RANDOLPH CALDECOTT
(1846-1886)

Born in Chester, UK. After leaving school he worked as a bank clerk while studying in the evenings at Manchester School of Art. There he met Thomas Armstrong who showed Caldecott's work to the editor of London Society magazine, who then published his first drawings in 1871. Caldecott's unfussy style, using strong outlines and flat areas of colour, was perfectly suited to children's book illustration and he was employed by the engraver Edmund Evans to take over the illustration of Routledge's Shilling Toybooks when his friend Walter Crane left after a quarrel about royalties. Caldecott had a particular love for the era that preceded the Industrial Revolution and his idealization of life in the country captured the hearts of the general public. Books illustrated include Washington Irving's Old Christmas (1875), The Diverting History of John Gilpin, The House That Jack Built (both 1878) and Three Jovial Huntsmen Sing a Song of Sixpence (1880). He also illustrated for Punch, Boy's Own Paper and The Graphic.

1

1 *NURSERY POSTER*
DATE: 1884

2, 3 *BOOK:* RANDOLPH CALDECOTT'S COLLECTION OF PICTURES AND SONGS *DATE: 1880*

2

3

1

*Born in Bromsgrove, UK.
Studied at Lambeth School of
Art and the Royal College of
Art. He began work as a book
illustrator, but when his eyesight
began to fail, turned to writing
adult books, plays and fairy
stories, which he illustrated
himself and published a great
deal on feminism, socialism and
pacifism. His bold use of black
and white shows the influence
of Aubrey Beardsley, but he
was also influenced by the
social realism of Dante Gabriel
Rossetti and others of the Pre-
Raphaelite Brotherhood. Books
illustrated include his own* The
Blue Moon *(1904), Christina
Rossetti's* Goblin Market *(1893)
and Shelley's* The Sensitive Plant
(1898).

1-4 *BOOK:* THE FIELD OF
CLOVER
DATE: 1898

2

3

4

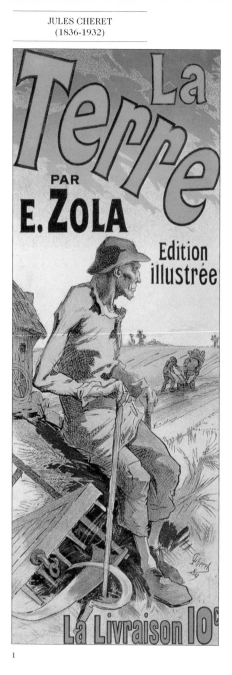

1

2

3

4

Born in Paris. After working as a lithographer he moved to London in 1859, to study the new techniques of printing in colour lithography being developed there, and earned his living designing book covers for Cramer Publishing and posters for the opera, circus and music hall. He also met and became the protégé of the perfumer Eugène Rimmel. In 1866 Rimmel provided the financial backing for Chéret to set up his own lithographic printing studio in Paris, from where he produced the first French posters printed in colour. His pioneering work in the development of chromolithography enabled the mass-production of posters and contributed to the development of the advertising poster as an artistic medium. His own posters capture the joie de vivre of the cabarets, music and dance halls, operas and theatres of Paris. He designed posters for the American dancer Loïe Fuller for her début at the Folies-Bergère, and his many images of lively dancing girls were popularly known as "Chérettes".

1 PUBLICITY POSTER: LATERRE by Emile Zola
DATE: 1889

2 POSTER: "LOÏE FULLER"
DATE: 1893

3 POSTER: "PALAIS DE GLACE"
DATE: 1896

4 POSTER: "JARDIN DE PARIS"
DATE: 1890

5 POSTER: "THEATRE DEL'OPERA"DATE: c. 1896

6 POSTER: "DANSEUSES ESPAGNOLES" DATE: c. 1896

5

6

Born in London. Studied at Heatherley's and the Slade School of Art, and began her career illustrating greetings cards. In 1877 she met the printer Edmund Evans, for whom she wrote and illustrated Under the Window *(1878). This was a great success and was followed by, among others,* The Birthday Book *(1880),* The Marigold Garden *(1885) and* The Pied Piper of Hamelin *(1888). She was encouraged in her career by John Ruskin, whom she befriended in 1882 and who, along with Gauguin and the public at large, was a great admirer of her simple style and nostalgic view of childhood.*

1 *PAINTING*
DATE: c. 1899

2 *BOOK:* MOTHER GOOSE
DATE: 1881

3 *FRONTISPIECE:* THE
MARIGOLD GARDEN
by Kate Greenaway
DATE: 1885

1

2

3

Born in Leeds, UK. He left
school at 13 and became an
assistant scene painter at the
Leeds Grand Theatre, where he
sold his drawings of the actors
and actresses for a shilling
each. At 14 he started drawing
for the Yorkshire Post and at
16 moved to London, where
he contributed to St Stephen's
Review. He then emigrated to
Australia and worked for three
years on the Sydney Bulletin.
Returning penniless to London,
he started the highly successful
"Parson and Painter" series
for St Stephen's Review, which
was published as a series of
annuals from 1891-1904. He
also drew for many periodicals,
including The Graphic, The
Daily Graphic and The Sketch.
In 1895 he joined the staff of
Punch, where he remained until
his death Sometimes referred
to as the "grandfather of British
illustration", he was regarded
by many as the most important
and influential black-and-white
artist of his generation. He lived
a bohemian life and died of
cirrhosis of the liver and TB at
the age of 39.

1 ADVERTISEMENT:
APOLLINARIS TABLE WATER
DATE: c. 1899

2 MAGAZINE: THE GRAPHIC
DATE: 1893

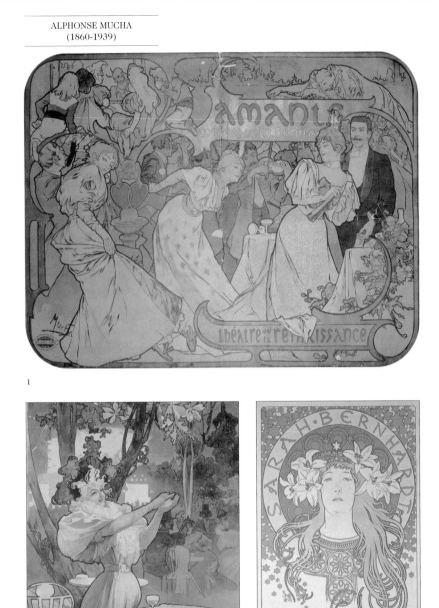

1

2

3

4

5

6

*Born in Czechoslovakia. Count
Karl Khuen Belasi commissioned
him to paint a series of murals
for his country home, and
subsequently financed Mucha's
studies at the Munich Academy.
The Count's suicide in 1889
was a financial blow to Mucha,
and he turned to illustrating
books and journals to make
a living. His rise to fame as a
leading Art Nouveau designer
began with a commission in
1894 to design a poster for
Sarah Bernhardt in her leading
role in* Gismonda. *The poster
so delighted Bernhardt that
she gave Mucha a six-year
contract to design posters,
stage sets, costumes, jewellery
and programmes for her
productions. During his career
Mucha designed many posters
and decorative panels, typically
featuring maidens in flowing
robes surrounded by formalized
decorative symbols. Between
1904 and 1912 he taught in New
York and Chicago, where his
work appeared in* The New York
Daily News *and* The Century
magazine.

1 *POSTER:* "LES AMANTS"
DATE: 1895

2 *POSTER:* "AU CAFÉ-
CONCERT"
DATE: 1900

3 *POSTER:* "SARAH
BERNHARDT"
DATE. c. 1900

4 *MAGAZINE COVER:*
L'ILLUSTRATION
DATE: 1896

5 *ADVERTISEMENT:* "JOB"
DATE: c. 1890

6 *ADVERTISEMENT:* RUINART
CHAMPAGNE
DATE. c. 1890

*Born in Albi, France. His
early talent for drawing was
encouraged by his uncle and
two family friends, the sporting
painters René Princeteau
and John Lewis Brown. After
studying art under Florentin
Léon Bonnat and at the school
of Fernand Cormon (where
he met Vincent van Gogh) he
was given an allowance in
1885 to set up his own studio
in the Montmartre district
of Paris. There he produced
his brilliant series of posters,
paintings and drawings
depicting popular singers,
dancers and scenes of Parisian
nightlife. Lautrec admired the
work of Degas and Gauguin,
and the current fashion for
Japanese art inspired his daring
layouts, bold outlines and solid
blocks of colour. In addition
to his posters, he produced
over 300 lithographs. He also
contributed to Courrier Français
and other Paris newspapers,
and illustrated Jules Renard's
Histoires Naturelles (1899).*

1

1 *POSTER:* "DIVAN JAPONAIS"
DATE: 1892

2 *POSTER:* "MAY BELFORT"
DATE: 1895

3 *POSTER:* "LAGOULUE"
DATE: 1892

4 *MAGAZINE:* LERIRE
DATE: 1895

5 *MAGAZINE:* LERIRE
DATE: 1896

2

3

4

5

Born in London. He was apprenticed to an engraver and subsequently opened a studio of his own and attended St Martin s Lane School. Using the name "Phiz", he illustrated most of the novels of Dickens, including Pickwick Papers *(1836),* Little Dorrit *(1857) and* Nicholas Nickleby *(1839). He contributed to various magazines, including* New Sporting Magazine, London Magazine, The Illustrated Times, Punch *and* The Illustrated London Magazine.

1 *BOOK:* LITTLE DORRIT *by Charles Dickens DATE: 1857*

1

1

HENRY HOLIDAY
(1839-19 27)

*Born in London. Studied at
Leigh's Academy and the Royal
Academy Schools. His interest in
the Pre-Raphaelite Brotherhood
led to his befriending Holman
Hunt and Burne-Jones, who had
a major influence on his work.
He is best known as a stained
glass artist, but achieved
fame as an illustrator for his
illustrations for Lewis Carroll's*
The Hunting of the Snark *(1876).*

1—4 *BOOK:* THE HUNTING OF
THE SNARK *by Lewis Carroll
DATE.* 1876

2

3

4

PIERRE BONNARD
(1867-1947)

Born in Paris. Studied painting at the Académie Julien in Paris in the late 1880s. With fellow students, including Maurice Denis and Edouard Vuillard he founded the Nabis, a group of artists with a shared interest in the graphic and decorative arts. In 1891 Bonnard's first commercial poster, France-Champagne, was published. Thereafter, posters, prints and book illustrations constituted a major part of his work for a number of years. His graphic oeuvre includes a set of lithographs entitled Aspects of the Life of Paris and illustrations for, among other works, Jules Renard's Histoires Naturelles (1904) and Octave Mirbeau's La 628 E 8 (1908), an account of an automobile trip through Europe. Subsequently Bonnard returned to the preoccupations of pure painting and is best known for the work of his later years, interior scenes suffused with colour and light.

1 EXHIBITION POSTER: "THE PRINT AND THE POSTER"
DATE: 1897

2 POSTER: "SALON DESCENT"
DATE: 1896

3 ADVERTISEMENT: LE FIGARO
DATE: c. 1899

1

2

3

"The enjoyment of Elinor's company"
Chapter XLIX

"You are extremely kind" replied Miss Bates.
Chapter XIX

1

2

"Of all the consequence in their power"
Chapter XX

3

*Born in Cambridge, UK.
Educated at Cambridge School
and in the studio of the sculptor
Henry Wiles. He shared a studio
with his younger brother, Henry
Matthew, and their work was
very similar, although Charles'
use of line was more tentative.
They were equally successful
and during their careers
illustrated most of the classics,
conjuring up images of "the
good old days" in the manner of
Hugh Thomson. Charles began
illustrating in 1891 and his
first major commission was for
Thomas Hoods* Humorous Poems
*(1893), which was very popular
and led to his most successful
book Swift's* Gulliver's Travels
(1894).

1 *BOOK:* SENSE AND
SENSIBILITY *by Jane Austen*
DATE: 1898

2 *BOOK:* PERSUASION
by Jane Austen
DATE: 1898

3 *BOOK:* EMMA *by Jane Austen*
DATE: 1898

CHAPTER TWO

AFTER THE DECADENCE OF THE FIN DE SIÉCLE Britain entered the 20th century with a fascination for the decorative arts, which found the perfect medium in the Edwardian gift book.

Many of these were children's stories, but the Net Book Agreement in 1900 had put an end to the booksellers' price war, and the increased cost of these volumes ensured that many if not most of them were for adult entertainment and not destined to suffer the clumsy attentions of boisterous children. Besides which, the subject matter was not of primary importance as the overriding concern was with the decorative possibilities of the book as a whole and not with a close interpretation of the text. The influence of Art Nouveau and Japanese art was extremely marked throughout this period, and the legacy of Aubrey Beardsley, who died in 1898 at the tragically young age of 23, continued to inspire. Beardsley's works were perfectly suited to the line block process, and there are those who believe he had no peers and that his style died with him. However, in the first decades of the 20th century, one can see his inspiration at work in the drawings of such artists as Alastair, Kay Nielson, Harry Clarke, Edmund Dulac and, to a lesser extent, Arthur Rackham, whose sepia-toned drawings have become definitive of the period. While Britain and Europe were in the grip of Art Nouveau, America was enjoying its own "golden age of illustration". In the 1890s Howard Pyle had injected a new lease of life into an otherwise dull period of children's illustration with his all-action, black-and-white drawings of adventure on the high seas. His pirate stories were immensely popular, and his prolific output was made possible by his habit of dictating the narrative to his secretary while working on the artwork at his easel.

However, Pyle's fame now rests more on the colour illustrations he did for magazines such as *Harper's* and on the extent of his influence as a teacher, a role that has earned him the title "the father of American illustration". He set up his own school at Chadd's Ford, Pennsylvania, where his star pupils were N C Wyeth, who produced a classic edition of *Treasure Island,* and Frank Schoonover, who inherited Pyle's Pre-Raphaelite obsession with authenticity as well as his love of the Wild West. But the influence of the Pyle school extended way beyond his pupils, and artists like Fred Remington travelled extensively to record the lives of trappers, cowboys and outbackers with a truthful and not romantic eye.

Of course, at that time America was also producing prominent artists who were outside of Pyle's sphere of influence—two examples being Maxfield Parrish and Charles Dana Gibson.

Parrish worked mainly for the major American magazines: *Harpers, Colliers, The Century* and *Life*. But the experimental nature of his work is beautifully captured in his illustrations for Kenneth Graham's *The Golden Age*, in which, using photographs as reference material, he recreated a child's view of the world by drawing it from a low eye level.

Charles Dana Gibson specialized in pen drawings of fashionable young women and his "Gibson Girls" made him famous and extremely rich. In 1904 *Collier's Weekly* offered him a four-year contract worth $100,000 (about £500,000 in today's terms). When you consider the staggering size of such a fee it is hardly surprising that magazines attracted the cream of American illustrative talent.

Throughout this period, while Europe dominated the field of book production, American publishers favoured the magazine. From an investor's point of view they were a safer bet, as sales could be predicted from fairly stable circulation figures, and the United States had superior technology that could withstand the constant pressure of deadlines while maintaining high standards of colour reproduction.

Gibson's eminence in this milieu is interesting, as it limited his interest to a particular subject matter. In the first decades of the 20th century, on both sides of the Atlantic, this sort of specialization became increasingly commonplace among illustrators. One only has to think of Louis Wain's cats, George Studdy's dogs, Cecil Aldin's horses, Bateman's outraged generals, J A Shepherd's animals clothed in human attire or Mabel Lucie Attwell's rosycheeked children to wonder whether this limiting of vision was a condition of the artist's imagination or the force of commerce sustaining a winning formula.

Certainly times were hard for most illustrators, and the arrival of poster and print advertising was a welcome opportunity for diversification. The economic depression after World War I led to a decline in the illustrated book market, but the 1920s and 1930s, particularly in Europe, saw dramatic developments in advertising art.

In Britain, Jack Beddington, the publicity manager of Shell, instigated some of the most famous advertising of all time and became an influential patron of the arts by commissioning the likes of Graham Sutherland, E McKnight Kauffer and Tom Purvis. On the Continent, advertising posters reached dizzying aesthetic heights in the work of the Futurist-inspired A M Cassandre.

This need for artists to find new outlets and media for their talents had been encouraged by the two World Wars. Propaganda to support these war efforts had been in heavy demand and some artists, such as James Montgommery Flagg in America, had become famous because of it. At the same time these conflicts encouraged the development of political and social satire, and illustration was broadly used to strengthen the voice of protest.

By the beginning of the 1940s the diversification of illustration had led the artist into every realm of human activity.

1

2

3

*Born in Nottingham, UK. He
left school at 11 to work as an
errand boy for a local milliner
and in 1886 was apprenticed to
a firm of lithographic printers
for no pay. After a year he was
earning one shilling a week.
At 17, he became interested in
cartoons and sent drawings
to the editor of 'Scraps comic,
which earned him 30 shillings.
At 19 he moved to London,
where he invented the popular
"Weary Willie" and "Tired Tim"
comic characters and went on to
work for the weekly illustrated
papers and Punch. He was a
member of the Royal Society
of British Artists and founder-
member of the London Sketch
Club. From 1904 he also enjoyed
some success in the USA with
a series of comic characters
called "Boston Types". He
contributed to numerous
magazines, including* Cycling,
The Wheel *and* Cycle Magazine,
*and designed posters for Raleigh
bicycles. He is most famous
for his advertising poster for
Johnnie Walker Whisky.*

1 *MAGAZINE:* THE POSTER
DATE: c. 1900

2 *ADVERTISEMENT:* FRY'S
CHOCOLATE
DATE: c. 1905

3. *ADVERTISEMENT:* FRY'S
CHOCOLATE
DATE: c. 1900

4 *ADVERTISEMENT:*
BEECHAM'S PILLS
DATE: c. 1905

4

*Born in London. She was
entirely self-taught as a water
colourist and displayed a
natural gift for drawing animals
from a very early age. Her
first book* The Tale of Peter
Rabbit, *was turned down by
several publishers, including
her subsequent publishers
Frederick Warne and Co., before
she published it at her own
expense in 1901. She published*
The Tailor of Gloucester *the
following year. Frederick Warne
then published revised versions
with illustrations in colour and
followed them with* The Tale of
Benjamin Bunny *(1904) and*
The Tale of Tom Kitten *(1907).
Nineteen books in the* Peter
Rabbit *series were to follow.
Beatrix Potter's little books,
with their delicate watercolour
vignettes and small blocks
of text have become part of
English nursery folklore. Her
animals, though endowed with
human attributes and dressed
in clothes, are nevertheless
real because they are sharply
observed from nature. She
cited the Pre-Raphaelites and
Randolph Caldecott as major
influences, and admired Mrs
Blackburn's bird and animal
illustrations as well as Thomas
Bewick's woodcuts.*

1, 2 *BOOK:* THE TALE OF
PETER RABBIT
DATE: 1901

3, 5 *BOOK:* THE TAILOR OF
GLOUCESTER
DATE: 1902

4 *BOOK:* THE TALE OF TOM
KITTEN
DATE: 1907

6 *BOOK:* THE TALE OF
BENJAMIN BUNNY
DATE: 1904

1

2

3

4

5

6

CHARLES DANA GIBSON
(1867-1944)

*Born in Massachusetts, USA.
Studied at the Art Students
League in New York and at
the Académie Julien in Paris.
Gibson quickly became an
international figure, famous
for his drawings chronicling
American high society, and
created a beautiful type of all-
American girl known as "the
Gibson Girl". He sold his first
drawing to Life magazine when
he was 19, beginning a lifelong
association which culminated
in his becoming its owner and
editor after World War I. An
early admirer of Abbey, Frost
and Pyle, he later developed
a special liking for the British
illustrators Charles Keene,
George du Maurier and Phil
May. He was President of the
Society of Illustrators during
World War I.*

1

1,2 BOOK: AMERICANS *by
Charles Dana Gibson*
DATE: 1901

2

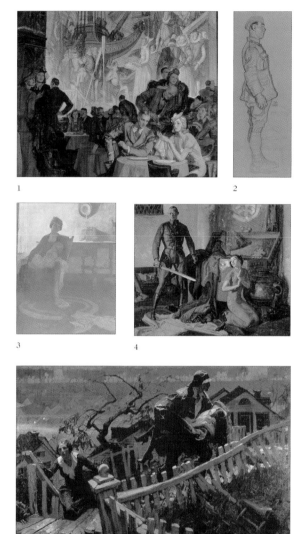

Cornwell was a student of Harvey
Dunn, through whom he inherited
much of the teaching of Howard
Pyle, and he also studied under
the muralist Frank Brangwyn.
Although obviously an exponent
of the Pyle school Cornwell's
style was more elaboratively
decorative. He worked in oils
and was painstaking in his
approach to the subject, making
many preliminary sketches, and
throughout the 1920s his beautiful
illustrations of swashbuckling
romantic costume dramas
dominated such magazines as
Redbook and Cosmopolitan.
However, it was Norman
Rockwell's belief that Cornwell's
best work was a series on the life
of Christ, for Good Housekeeping,
which he painted after a trip
to the Middle East. His murals
are no less impressive than his
illustrations, the most notable
being those for the Los Angeles
Public Library, the Lincoln
Memorial in California and the
Tennessee State Office Building.
He taught illustration at the Art
Students League in New York,
where he created the "Cornwell
School", and had a profound
influence on such artists as
Harry Beckhoff Dan Content,
Rico Tomaso, Robert Benney and
Frank Reilly. From 1922-26 he
was President of the Society of
Illustrators and was elected to its
Hall of Fame in 1959.

1 MAGAZINE: COSMOPOLITAN
DATE: 1923

2. DRAWING: WWI "DOUGHBOY"
DATE: c. 1918

3 MAGAZINE: COSMOPOLITAN
DATE: c. 1918

4 PAINTING DATE: 1938

5 MAGAZINE: COSMOPOLITAN
DATE: 1923

Born in London. Edward and his twin brother Charles Maurice started drawing in early childhood and, though neither had received any formal training both exhibited at the Royal Academy from the age of 14. They collaborated on several books, including Pictures from Birdland *(1899) and Kipling's* The Jungle Book *(1903), until Charles Maurice committed suicide in 1908 at the age of 25. Alone, Edward illustrated* The Fables of Aesop *(1909), Fabres* Book of Insects *(1921) and* The Arabian Nights *(Tales From One Thousand and One Nights) (1924), which shows the strong influence of Japanese prints and Eastern miniature painting. He specialized in drawing animals and plants, often placed in fantastical settings.*

1, 2 *BOOK:* THE JUNGLE BOOK
by Rudyard Kipling
DATE: 1903

3 *BOOK:* HOURS OF GLADNESS
by M Maeterlinck
DATE: 1912

4, 5 *BOOK:* OUR LITTLE
NEIGHBOURS, ANIMALS OF
THE FARM AND WOOD
DATE: 1921

1

2

3

4

5

CHARLES MARION RUSSELL
(1864-1926)

*Born in Missouri, USA. Russell's
childhood interest in drawing
cowboys and Indians was to
shape his life. He left school at
16 and worked as a cowboy,
then as a fur-trapper. In 1888 he
spent six months living with the
Blackfoot Indians and learned
to communicate with them in
sign language. As an artist he
was entirely self-taught. His
wife Nancy encouraged him to
become a full-time illustrator,
handling his finances and
organising his commissions.
His work appeared in
many magazines, including*
Recreation, Western Field,
Sports Afield *and* Outing, *and
he later contributed to* Scribner'
s, McClures *and* The Saturday
Evening Post. *A contemporary of
Fred Remington, his beautifully
coloured paintings captured
the spirit of the life he depicted
and showed a remarkable
understanding of animal
anatomy. He was elected
posthumously to the Illustrators'
Hall of Fame in 1985.*

1 *PAINTING:* "COWBOYS
ROPING A STEER"
DATE; c. 1900

2 *PAINTING:* "COWBOYS
ROPING A STEER"
DATE: 1904

1

2

1

Born in London. He had no
formal training, but learned
his art while working for
the magazine Moonshine,
developing a particular talent
for drawing birds and animals
in pen and ink, which became
his speciality. Although comic
and usually clothed in human
attire, his creatures are
nevertheless entirely plausible
characters, his illustrations
for Uncle Remus (1901)
being excellent examples. He
had a long association with
Punch magazine from 1893
and drew for several other
magazines, including The
Sporting and Dramatic News
and Cassell's Family Magazine.
His caricatures for The Strand
Magazine, known as "Zig-Zags",
proved so popular that they
were subsequently published as
a book, Zig-Zag Fables, in 1897.
Other books include The Three
Jovial Puppies (1907) and The
Life of a Foxhound (1910).

1—3 *BOOK:* UNCLE REMUS
by J Chandler Harris
DATE: 1901

2   3

1

2

3

4

5

6

7

Born in Auckland, New Zealand, the son of a banker. He worked as a lithographer before moving to London in 1901. His humorous drawings of animals and children were commissioned by Little Folks, The Humorist, Playtime *and* Punch. *He became one of the most successful children's illustrators of his day and in 1914 was President of the London Sketch Club. Books illustrated include* Alice in Wonderland *(1908),* Alice Through the Looking Glass *(1928) and* The Magic Wand *(1908). Among his own works were* Birds, Beasts and Fishes *(1929) and* Rabbit Rhymes *(1934). He also illustrated for magazines such as* The Sketch, The Graphic *and* The Strand Magazine.

1- 4 *BOOK:* UNCLE REMUS
by J Chandler Harris
DATE: 1906

---

5 *ORIGINAL PRINT*
DATE: NOT KNOWN

6,7 *BOOK:* AESOP'S FABLES
DATE: 1924

1

Christian passes through the Valley of the Shadow of Death.

Little biographical detail is known about this artist, but he was a prolific illustrator with an expert understanding of the various reproduction media His finely drawn line work appeared in The Children of the Dawn *(1908),* The Book of Psalms *(1912) and* The Story Without an End *(1912). He illustrated classics from* The Pilgrim's Progress *(1910) to* Tales from the Arabian Nights *(1934) and also contemporary novels, and contributed to* The Boy's Herald, Cassell's Magazine *and* The Pall Mall Magazine. *His illustrations to six works by Anatole France, produced in the 1920s, are regarded as among his finest and he became something of a cult figure during that period.*

His wife, Agnes Stringer, collaborated with him on some projects, providing the colour work to his drawings.

1 *BOOK:* THE PEDLAR AND HIS DOG *by Mary C Rowsell*
DATE: 1922

2-5 *BOOK:* THE PILGRIM'S PROGRESS *by John Bunyan*
DATE: c. 1909

2

There came to him a Hand with some of the leaves of the tree of life.

Christian and Hopeful under the power of Giant Despair.

Christian on his way to Begality's house.

3   4   5

Born in London. Attended the
West London School of Art,
1877-80, and taught there
during the following two years.
Encouraged by his wife, Emily,
he sold his first drawing of a cat
(based on his own, Peter) to The
Illustrated London News in 1884.
His first book, Madam Tabby's
Establishment (1886), made
him a household name as "the
man who drew cats", and in
1890 he was made President of
the National Cat Club, devising
their coat of arms and motto.
From 1890, Wain invented
a world of "humanize" cats,
sporting top hats and monocles,
playing tennis and drinking tea.
The public loved them, and Wain
was approached to illustrate
countless books, articles and
picture postcards. In 1907 he
went to New York, where he
drew a cat strip cartoon for
New York American. In 1917
he produced an animated film,
Pussyfoot, with the pioneer film-
maker HF Wood. The first Louis
Wain Annual appeared in 1901
and annuals appeared regularly
until 1921, when the public
appetite for Wain's drawings
diminished. Diagnosed as
schizophrenic at the age of 63,
he spent his last years at the
Royal Bethlem Hospital in south
London.

1

2

3

1 "CATS'TEA PARTY"
(unpublished)
DATE: c. 1910

2 "THE CHAIRMAN"
(unpublished)
DATE: c. 1910

3 POSTCARD
DATE: NOT KNOWN

Born in Mossac, France. Brother of the artist Felix François Bouisset, he was a painter, engraver and illustrator. His style was very much of the Art Nouveau period and he is best remembered for his paintings of children and for his posters, most notably those for Meunier chocolate and Job papers. His work also appeared in the publications Le Capitan *(1833) and* L'Estampe Moderne *(1899) and his illustrated books include* Lajournée de Bébé *(1885) and* Les Bébés d'Alsace de Lorraine *(1886). He died in Paris at the age of 66.*

1 "LABOUQUETIÉRE"
(unpublished)
DATE: c. 1900

2 *POSTER:* "LONDON COUNTRY & WESTMINSTER BANK (PARIS) LTD"
DATE: 1919

3 *ADVERTISEMENT:* "CHOCOLAT DE L'UNION"
DATE: c. 1900

1

2

3

HOWARD PYLE
(1853-1911)

*Born in Delaware, USA and
educated at the Art Students
League in New York. Pyle is
often referred to as "the father of
American illustration", because
of the enormous influence both
of his work and his teaching.
He taught at the Drexel Institute
in Philadelphia and then at the
Art Students League in New
York before setting up his own
art schools at Chadd's Ford,
Pennsylvania, and Wilmington,
Delaware, where no fees were
charged. Some of his star pupils
included N C Wyeth, Frank
Schoonover and Jessie Wilcox
Smith. Books illustrated include*
The Merry Adventures of Robin
Hood *(1883), a series of books
which he also wrote re-telling
the legends of King Arthur, and*
Book of Pirates *(1902). He also
contributed to a number of
magazines, including* Harpers.

1—3 *BOOK:* HOWARD PYLE'S
BOOK OF PIRATES
DATE. 1902

4 *MAGAZINE:* HARPER'S
MONTHLY
DATE. 1911

5 *MAGAZINE:* HARPER'S
MONTHLY
DATE: 1906

1

2

3

4

5

EL LISSITZKY
(1890-1941)

*Born in Smolensk, Russia.
Studied in Germany and took up
book illustration on his return
to Russia in 1912. He illustrated
seven children's books,
including* The Kid *(1917), which
revealed the influence of Marc
Chagall,* Ukrainian Fairy Tales
(1919) and The Four Billygoats
*(1924). In 1919 he entered
what he termed his "Proun"
period—the name he gave to
his abstract style and which
was an acronym meaning
"Project for the Establishment
of the New Art". In 1920 he
produced* Of Two Squares, *an
abstract play book for children
that showed a red square
attacking and defeating a black
square. In 1921 he returned to
Germany, where he was deeply
impressed by the Dadaists and
Expressionists, and in 1925
wrote* The Isms of Art *with Hans
Arp. Throughout his career
he was a highly influential
political artist, famous for his
posters and his geometric use of
typography. He designed the first
flag of the Central Committee
of the Communist Party of the
Soviet Union and between 1932
and 1937 created a series of
montages called "Building the
USSR", which bring to mind the
work of John Heartfield.*

1, 2 *BOOK: (published in
Russia)*
*DATE.*1923

3 *BOOK: (published in Russia)*
DATE: 1916

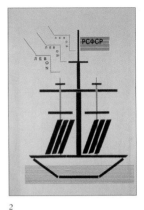

1   2

3

The Banquet

1

Born in Boston, USA He started
work at the age of 12 on a
Michigan newspaper and in
1895 illustrated his first book,
Fringilla by R D Blackmore,
which clearly shows the
influence of Beardsley and Art
Nouveau. In the same year
he founded his own Wayside
Press Company, in Springfield,
Massachusetts, and developed
his interest in typography
and book design. He wrote,
illustrated and produced Peter
Poodle: Toy Maker to the King
(1906) and Launcelot and the
Ladies (1927). He was also a
talented poster designer, and
was art director of Collier's,
Metropolitan and The Century
magazines.

1 *BOOK:* PETER POODLE: TOY
MAKER TO THE KING
DATE: 1906

2 *POSTER*
DATE: c. 1920

3 *BOOK JACKET:* THE CHAP
BOOK *by Will Bradley*
DATE: NOT KNOWN

2

3

LUDWIG HOHLWEIN
(1874-1949)

Born in Wiesbaden, Germany. Trained as an architect and practised until 1906, with a special interest in exhibition design. He was self-taught as an artist, but his first poster design, a sporting guns advertisement, won him immediate recognition. His personal interest in hunting field sports and animal life was frequently reflected in the style and content of his commercial work. Whether for tailoring or perfumes, tobacco or confectionery, or the circus, his posters show his confident handling of form, colour and pattern, assembled into bold and inventive imagery. In a poster for Grathwohl cigarettes (1921), the product is represented only by a tiny red glow at the mouth of a silhouetted figure; frequently figures appear as outlined shapes filled with solid blocks of colour and pattern. In later work, high tonal contrasts and a network of interlocking shapes provide modelling of three-dimensional forms. His style is unmistakable and was powerfully adapted to propagandist posters in both World Wars.

1

1 *ADVERTISEMENT:* PKZ
DATE: 1908

2 *ADVERTISEMENT:* MACHOLL
COGNAC
DATE: c. 1910

3 *ADVERTISEMENT:* RIQUETTA
DATE: c 1910

4 *WWI POSTER:* "THE
LUDENDORFF FUND FOR THE
WAR WOUNDED"
DATE: 1917

2

3

4

EDMUND DULAC
(1882-1953)

*Born in Toulouse, France. He
took evening classes in art
while studying law at Toulouse
University, and won a scholarship
to the Académie Julien in Paris, but
left after three weeks to concentrate
on his career as an illustrator. He
was an Anglophile from childhood
(his nickname at school was
"l'Anglais") and settled in London
in 1905. By the time he became
a naturalized British subject in
1912, he was established as one
of the leading artists in his field.
During World War I he designed
charity stamps and later Jubilee
and Coronation stamps and was
commissioned by Charles de
Gaulle to design posters, bank
notes and postage stamps. He
was a friend of WB Yeats, many
of whose works he illustrated,
and collaborated with him on
a production of* At the Hawk's
Well, *composing the music and
designing the costumes, sets and
make-up. Books illustrated include*
Stories of the Arabian Nights,
*retold by Laurence Housman
(1907),* Shakespeare's The Tempest
(1908), Stories from Hans Christian
Andersen *(1911) and the novels of
the Brontë sisters in ten volumes
(1905). Dulac's brilliant use of flat
colour owes a great deal to the
influence of Japanese prints and
his passionate interest in Persian
miniatures.*

1   2

3

---

1 *BOOK-* KING ALBERT
DATE: 1914

---

2 *PAINTING:* "THE
ENTOMOLOGIST"
DATE: 1909

---

3 *BOOK:* THE MERMAID KING *by
Hans Christian Andersen
DATE:* 1911

---

4 *CARICATURE:* SIR EDWARD
PENISONROSS
DATE: 1915

4

HENRY MATTHEW BROCK
(1875-1960)

Born in Cambridge, UK, younger brother of Charles Edmund Brock. Studied at Cambridge School of Art. He illustrated for numerous periodicals, including The Graphic, Punch *and* The Sketch. *Books illustrated include Walter Scott's* Ivanhoe *(1900), Defoe's* Robinson Crusoe *(1904), Hans Andersen's* Fairy Tales and Stories *(1905), Dent's* The Novels of Jane Austen *and R L Stevenson's* Treasure Island *(1928). He also designed posters for the D'Oyly Carte during the 1920s. Brock worked almost entirely in pen and ink. His flair for drama and action, and his fluent and vigorous line, made him popular as an illustrator of boys' stories. He was described by the illustrator A E Bestall as "probably the last of the era of perfectionists".*

1-3 *BOOK:* THE BOOK OF FAIRY TALES
DATE: 1914

1

2

3

1

2

Born in Bradford UK. Studied at
Bradford School of Art and the
Royal College of Art, London. He
began work as a portrait painter
but went on to a successful
career as an illustrator of
children's books He contributed
illustrations to children's stories
in The Graphic and book titles
include Tales for Tiny Tots and
The Rock-a-Bye Stories (1919),
The Woodland Series (1919),
Famous Animal Tales (1935) and
The Brambledown Tales (1946).
His work was published in the
USA, Canada and Australia as
well as in the UK.

1 BOOK: THE TREASURE
SEEKERS by E Nesbit
DATE: 1917

2 BOOK: THE HOUSE THAT
JACK BUILT (traditional rhyme)
DATE: 1920

3 POSTER: LONDON UNITED
TRAMWAYS
DATE: 1915

4 POSTER: LONDON UNITED
TRAMWAYS
DATE: 1915

THE LONDON UNITED TRAMWAYS

THE PHEASANT AT HOME

TO PAY YOUR RESPECTS
TRAVEL BY TRAM TO THE

BUCKINGHAMSHIRE WOODS AT
UXBRIDGE

3

THE LONDON UNITED TRAMWAYS

THE KINGFISHER AT HOME

TO PAY YOUR RESPECTS
TRAVEL BY TRAM TO THE
RIVERSIDE AT . . . . .

HAMPTON COURT OR
KEW BRIDGE

4

Born in London. Trained at Westminster School of Art and the Royal Academy Schools. He also studied under Sir George Frampton in England and Morot in Paris. Books illustrated include Jack the Giant Killer *and* Beauty and the Beast *and* The Sleeping Beauty *and* Dick Whittington *(both published in 1894),* Poems *by John Keats (1897), Shelley's* Poems *(1902), Shakespeare's* The Tempest *(1901) and, his most successful book,* A Midsummer Night's Dream *(1895). He also contributed to* The Yellow Book *quarterly. Bell's work was firmly rooted in the Arts and Crafts tradition, often featuring long, angular figures, without shading contained within decorative borders. As well as being an illustrator, he was also a sculptor and designer of stained glass and mosaics. (Examples of his mosaics may be seen at the Houses of Parliament and at Westminster Cathedral.)*
He taught at Liverpool Municipal College, the Glasgow School of Art and the Royal College of Art, and became a member of the Royal Academy in 1922.

1 *BOOK:* DAILY CHRONICLE
PORTFOLIO
DATE: 1911

2 *BOOK PLATE*
DATE: 1910

3 *BOOK:* PALGRAVE'S GOLDEN
TREASURY
DATE: c. 1914

1

2

3

1

Born in Stuttgart, Germany. Mainly self taught, in 1905 he won a competition sponsored by the Berlin Chamber of Commerce with a poster for Priester matches, an image which set the hallmark of his style – descriptively economical shapes, bold colours and the strong presence of the brand name – later applied to posters for Stiller shoes, Manoli cigarettes, Osrnm lamps and Adler typewriters. This concentration on the advertised product, eliminating all other elements that might distract, became known as sachplakat (object-poster). During World War I, Bemhards expertise was applied to war propaganda posters. In 1920 he became the first Professor of Poster Design at the (then) Royal Academy in Berlin, and with Dr Hans Sachs he established the magazine Das Plakat. In 1923 he moved to the USA, where he became a founder-member of the New York design firm Contempora, Inc., with Rockwell Kent and others. His design skills were applied to trademarks, packaging emblems and printers' ornaments, and he is well known for type design, with 36 typefaces to his credit, including Bernhard-Antigua and Fraktur.

1 *WWI POSTER:* WAR LOAN
DATE: 1917

2 *ADVERTISEMENT:*
BENEDICTINE LIQUEUR
DATE: 1921

3 *ADVERTISEMENT:* OIGEE
BINOCULARS
DATE: 19071

2

3

EMIL CARDINAUX
(1877-1937)

Born in Berne, Switzerland. He began drawing as a child and by the age of 18 he had already illustrated The Legend of William Tell. *He studied art under Paul Volmars at Berne University and in 1898 studied under Franz Stuck at the Munich Art Academy. He travelled and lived in various parts of Europe and from 1903-04 worked as an artist in France and Italy. His versatile technique enabled him to succeed as a caricaturist illustrator and poster designer.*

1 *TRAVEL POSTER:* ZERMATT
DATE: 1908

2 *TRAVEL POSTER:* DAVOS
DATE: 1918

3 *TRAVEL POSTER:*
LOTSCHBERG
DATE: c. 1916

4 *POSTER:* "SWISS COUNTY
EXHIBITION, BERNE"
DATE: 1914

1

2

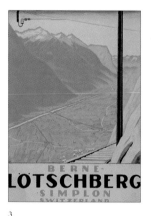

3

4

1

2

*Born in Copenhagen, Denmark
He spent his childhood
surrounded by artists, writers
and musicians, among them
Ibsen and Grieg. His early talent
for drawing was encouraged
by his parents and at the age of
17 he was sent to the Académie
Julien in Paris, where he came
under the influence of Art
Nouveau, Japanese art, and
the work of Aubrey Beardsley.
His first commission was for* In
Powder and Crinoline *(1913),
which was later published as*
Twelve Dancing Princesses *in
the USA. He also illustrated* One
Thousand and One Nights *(1918-
22),* East of the Sun and West
of the Moon *(1914) and* Hans
Andersen's Fairy Tales *(1924).
Nielsen was a brilliant colourist
whose intensely decorative
style came under a number of
influences, including Beardsley,
"Alastair", Vernon Hill, Middle
Eastern art and the sculptural
effects of the incipient Art Deco.
After exhibiting in New York in
1917 he emigrated to the USA
in 1922, moving to Hollywood
in 1939, where he designed for
a number of film companies,
including Walt Disney.*

1 *BOOK:* THE KING ALBERT
BOOK
DATE: 1914

2, 3 *BOOK:* IN POWDER AND
CRINOLINE
DATS: 1913

3

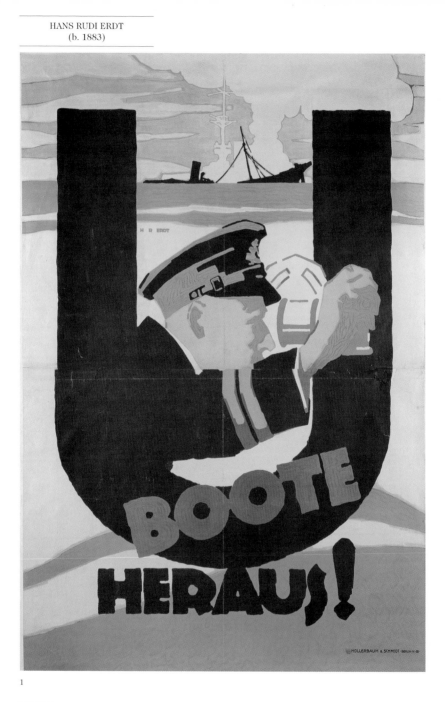

1

1

MOTHERS-VOTE LABOUR

2

YESTERDAY-THE TRENCHES

Born in South Bavaria. After leaving grammar school he studied at the Industrial Art College in Munich, where he was the protégé of his professor, Maximilian von Dasio. In 1905 he moved to Berlin, where he became a commercial poster artist. His style tended towards two-dimensional caricatures and his early work shows the influence of Ludwig Hohlwein, whereas in his later drawings one can see his admiration for the compositions and technique of Lucian Bernhard.

1 POSTER
DATE: 1917

"WORKLESS"

3

PAGEANT OF EMPIRE, WEMBLEY
21ST JULY TO 30TH AUGUST, 1924

The Abundance of Africa
EVERY EVENING
21ST JULY TO 9TH AUGUST AT 8·0 p.m.
11TH AUGUST TO 30TH AUGUST AT 7·30 p.m.

4

GERALD SPENCER PRYSE
(1882-1956)
Born in Ashton, UK. He studied art in London and Paris, became a member of the International Society and exhibited at Venice from 1907. He lived in Morocco from 1950 until his death. His illustrations appeared in Punch, The Strand Magazine *and* The Graphic.

1 POSTER
DATE: c. 1919

2 POSTER
DATE: c. 1919

3 POSTER
DATE: c. 1919

4 POSTER
DATE: 1924

Born in London. Attended
evening classes at Lambeth
School of Art while working as
a clerk. By 1891 he was selling
illustrations to The Pall Mall
Gazette, Scraps and Illustrated
Bits, and in 1892 he joined the
staff of The Westminster Budget
Magazine. Rodham was one of
the foremost Edwardian book
illustrators, specializing in tales
with a mystical, magical or
legendary theme. Until 1905 he
was highly regarded as a line
illustrator, but the introduction
of colour printing in the early
1900s enabled him also to use
the subtle tints and muted tones
for which he is now so widely
known. He was influenced by
Doyle, Houghton and Beardsley,
as well as the prints of Dürer
and Altdorfer. He illustrated
over 50 books, including The
Fairy Tales of the Brothers
Grimm (1900), Rip Van Winkle
(1905), Alice in Wonderland
(1907), The Arthur Rackham
Fairy Book (1933), Christina
Rossetti's Goblin Market (1933),
Edgar Allan Poe's Tales of
Mystery and Imagination (1935)
and Kenneth Grahame's The
Wind in the Willows (1940).

1

2

1 ORIGINAL DESIGN: THE
HOUSE THAT JACK BUILT
(traditional rhyme)
DATE: 1913

2 BOOK: PEER GYNT
by Henrik Ibsen
DATE: 1936

3 SOURCE: NOT KNOWN
DATE: NOT KNOWN

4 BOOK: THE NIGHT BEFORE
CHRISTMAS by C C Moore
DATE: 1931

5 BOOK: PETER PAN IN
KENSINGTON GARDENS
by J M Barrie
DATE: 1906

3

4

5

FRED REMINGTON
(1861-1909)

Born in New York State. He was educated for a short while at Yak University before going west to work as a cowboy, where he began drawing images of the disappearing Wild West. The early drawings which he sent to Harpers *magazine were published only after being redrawn by staff artists, but his work improved and he eventually joined the magazine staff himself. Books illustrated include* Ranch Life and the Hunting Trail *(1888) by his friend Theodore Roosevelt, and Longfellow's* The Song of Hiawatha *(1891).*

1 *PAINTING:* "STAMPEDED BY LIGHTNING"
DATE: 1908

2 *PAINTING:* "SMOKE SIGNALS"
DATE. 1905

1

2

1

2

3

Born in Neuenburg Switzerland. Studied fine art at the art school in La Chaux-de-Fonds under Georges Aubert and at the Académie Julien in Paris. He began his career as an illustrator for various Parisian publishing companies, and from 1906 he illustrated books and worked for the Geneva Tribune newspaper. His favourite themes were circus and racing horses, which he both painted and sculpted. His brilliant use of colour and typography ensured his success as a poster artist and his work for various clients covered a broad range of subjects.

1 *POSTER:* "20th ANNIVERSARY OF THE REVIVAL OF THE OLYMPIC GAMES"
DATE: 1914

2 *TRAVEL POSTER:* WINTER SPORTS, FRANCE
DATE: 1905

3 *TRAVEL POSTER:* NEUCHATEL, SWITZERLAND
DATE: 1914

HUGH THOMSON
(1860-1920)

Born in Londonderry, Northern Ireland. He began work at the age of 17 designing Christmas cards for Messrs Marcus Ward in Belfast. He moved to London in 1883 and became a regular contributor to The English Illustrated magazine. Thomson was a great admirer of E A Abbey, whose influence can be seen in his excellent black-and-white drawings, which perfectly captured the period details of the stories he illustrated. From the mid-1880s, his work graced the pages of novels by authors such as Goldsmith, Jane Austen, Sheridan and Mrs Gaskell.

His first major success was Tristram's Coaching Days and Coaching Ways (1888), followed in 1891 by the even more successful Vicar of Wakefield by Oliver Goldsmith. Other books illustrated include Goldsmith's She Stoops To Conquer (1912), J M Barrie's Quality Street (1913) and several Shakespeare plays. He also illustrated for most of the major magazines, including Black & White, The Pall Mall Budget and The Graphic. A pioneer of the new photomechanical process in the early 1900s, Thomson did his best work between 1900 and 1915 and was enormously influential on a whole generation of younger artists.

1 BOOK: QUALITY STREET by
J M Barrie
DATE: 1913

2 BOOK: EMMA by Jane Austen
DATE: c. 1900

3 BOOK: THE MERRY WIVES
OF WINDSOR by William
Shakespeare
DATE: 1910

1

2

3

1

Born in New York of English
parentage. Studied in New York,
Paris and Holland. Initially
she was a portrait painter,
but in 1893 she began making
sketches of the wooden dolls she
had played with as a child. She
invented the name "Golliwogg"
for her favourite and in 1895 she
illustrated a picture book of his
adventures, with simple rhymes
written by her mother. The
Adventures of Two Dutch Dolls
and a Golliwogg, with its brightly
coloured whole-page drawings
and hand-written text, was a
great success and led to a series
of thirteen Golliwogg books,
including The Golliwogg in War!
(1899), The Golliwogg's Auto Go-
Cart (1901) and The Golliwogg's
Fox Hunt (1905). The original
manuscripts and the doll itself
were auctioned for charity and
are now kept at Chequers, the
country home of British Prime
Ministers.

1 *BOOK:* THE GOLLIWOGG'S
AUTO GO- CART
DATE: 1901

2 *ADVERTISEMENT:*
WELLINGTON BROMIDE
PAPERS
DATE: c. 1910

3 *ADVERTISEMENT:*
WELLINGTON CELLULOID
FILM
DATE: c. 1910

2

3

ENRIETTE WILLEBEEK LEMAIR
(1889-1966)

(Baroness H van Tuyllvan Serooskerken.) Born in Rotterdam, Holland. Her parents were patrons of the arts and on the advice of the French illustrator Maurice Boutet de Monvel (by whose work she was deeply influenced), she was educated at the Rotterdam Academy. Her first British book, Our Old Nursery Rhymes, *was published in 1911 and over the next two decades her delicate pastel illustrations of children became increasingly popular. Her work appeared in* Old Dutch Nursery Rhymes *(1917), A A Milne's* A Gallery of Children *(1925) and RL Stevenson's* A Child's Garden of Verses *(1926). Her interest in a child's world extended beyond illustration as she also designed children's tableware.*

1–3 *BOOK:* OUR OLD NURSERY RHYMES
DATE: 1911

1 ORANGES AND LEMONS

2 HERE WE GO ROUND THE MULBERRY BUSH

3 HICKORY DICKORY DOCK

1

2

3

1

2

3

4

Born in London, the brother
of William Heath Robinson.
He won a scholarship to the
Royal Academy Schools but
was financially unable to take
it up. Instead he worked as an
apprentice printer during the
day and attended art classes
in the evenings. In 1895 his
illustrations were printed in The
Studio magazine, which led to
his being invited to illustrate R
L Stevenson's A Child's Garden
of Verse (1895). He subsequently
illustrated well over a hundred
books, mostly for children,
including Lewis Carroll's Alice's
Adventures in Wonderland
(1907), The Big Book of Fairy
Tales (1911) and Oscar Wilde's
The Happy Prince and Other
Stories (1913). He illustrated for
magazines including Black &
White, The Graphic, The Queen
and The Yellow Book. Robinson
painted delicate and sensitive
watercolours, and his black and
white illustrations, reflecting
the influence of Beardsley, Dürer
and Walter Crane, made him as
famous in his day as Beardsley
had been in his.

1 BOOK: THE SENSITIVE
PLANT by Percy Shelley
DATE: 1911

2-4 BOOK: THE HAPPY PRINCE
AND OTHER STORIES by Oscar
Wilde
DATE: 1913

Born in Philadelphia, USA.
He worked as a clerk while
taking evening classes at
the Pennsylvania School of
Industrial Art, until he was
expelled for leading a student
rebellion in 1879. He attended
the Pennsylvania Academy of
Fine Arts, but left in 1880 to
become a freelance illustrator
and writer. He married
Elizabeth Robins, the authoress,
and they settled in England in
1884. There the Pennells wrote
a biography of their friend, the
artist James McNeill Whistler,
and also brought the young
illustrator Aubrey Beardsley
to public attention with an
article on his work in the first
edition of The Studio magazine.
Pennell lectured in illustration
at the Slade School of Art and
the Royal College and won
many awards, including gold
medals at the Paris and Dresden
Expositions. His illustrations
appeared in magazines such as
The Yellow Book, The Graphic,
The English Illustrated and Pall
Mall. Books illustrated include
The Jew At Home (1892) and
Henry James's A Little Tour
in France (1900), as well as
numerous travel books written
by his wife.

THAT LIBERTY SHALL NOT
PERISH FROM THE EARTH
BUY LIBERTY BONDS
FOURTH   LIBERTY   LOAN

1

1 *WWI POSTER:* "BUY LIBERTY
BONDS"
DATE: 1917

2 *ENGRAVING*
DATE: 1909

3 *ENGRAVING*
DATE: 1911

2   3

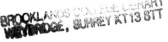

Real name: Baron Hans Henning Voight. Born in Karlsruhe, Germany. Self-taught as an artist, he was also a dancer, mime artist, pianist and writer. His career as a graphic artist was launched in 1914, when John Lane published Forty-Three Drawings by Alastair. *He also illustrated Oscar Wilde's* The Sphinx *(1920), Edgar Allan Poe's* The Fall of the House of Usher *(1928), Choderlos de Laclos's* Les Liaisons Dangereuses *(1929) and his own* Fifty Drawings by Alastair *(1925). Like Beardsley, whom he greatly admired, Alastair's illustrations combined decorative elegance with a fascination for the perverse and the sinister. His drawings, in black and white and sometimes coloured ink, were compositions inspired by novels, poems, plays or figures of legend or history. He exhibited at the Weyhe Gallery in New York in 1925.*

1 *BOOK:* THE SPHINX
by Oscar Wilde
DATE: 1920

1

*Born in Oxford, New Jersey,
USA. Studied under Howard
Pyle at the Drexel Institute and
then at Pyle's school at Chadd's
Ford, Pennsylvania. He studied
hard and the influence of Pyle
as mentor is evident both in his
painterly style and his choice of
subject matter. Both men had
a love of the colonial Past and
the Wild West and Schoonover
subscribed to Pyle's view that
an illustrator must be closely
invoked with the subject
of his work. To this end he
travelled widely and in difficult
circumstances to record the
lives of cowboys, Indians and
Eskimos. His work appeared
in* Arctic Stowaways *(1917)*,
Ivanhoe *(1922)*, J W Schultz's
Questers of the Desert *(1925)*,
M P Smith's Boy Captives of
Old Deerfield *(1929) and V M
Collier's* Roland the Warrior
(1934), among others.

1

---

1 *PAINTING:* "BELLEAU WOOD"
DATE: 1918

---

2 *ADVERTISEMENT:* COLT'S
FIREARMS
*DATE.*1925

---

3 *BOOK:* JOAN OF ARC
DATE: 1920

2

3

1

Born in Scotland. Studied
at Glasgow School of Art,
where she later taught, and
at the Royal College of Art in
London. An early member of
the "Glasgow School", with
Charles Rennie Mackintosh, she
was very much apart of the Art
Nouveau movement. Her style is
often attributed to the influence
of Aubrey Beardsley, but the
delicacy of her line and colour
was very much the product of
her own imaginative world,
populated as it was by her real
belief in fairies. In 1902 she won
a gold medal far her drawings
at the Turin International
Exhibition of Modern Decorative
Art. Her illustrated books
include William Morris's The
Defence of Queen Guinevere and
Other Poems (1906), Milton's
Comus (1906) and Oscar
Wilde's A House of Pomegranates
(1915), after which there was a
noticeable strengthening in her
use of both line and colour. She
also illustrated far a number
of magazines, including The
Studio.

1 BOOK: PONTSDE PARIS
BATE: 1912

2 BOOK: THE STUDIO
DATE: 1919

2

*Born in Philadelphia, USA.
Studied at the Pennsylvania
Academy of Fine Art under
Thomas Eakins, and at the
Drexel Institute under Howard
Pyle. Abandoning her original
plans to be a kindergarten
teacher, she concentrated
instead on a career as an
illustrator. She became very
successful, especially with
her portrayals of mothers and
babies and children at work
and at play, and illustrated a
number of books, including
Robert Louis Stevenson's* A
Child's Garden of Verses *(1905),
Charles Kingsley's* The Water
Babies *(1911), Johanna Spyri's*
Heidi *(1922), a US edition of*
Alice in Wonderland *and Louisa
M Alcott's* Little Women *(1915).
She also worked for a number
of advertising clients, and
contributed to Ladies'* Home
Journal, Collier's, Harper's,
Scribner's *and* The Century.
*From 1918 to 1932 her pictures
of adorable, beautifully dressed
children appeared monthly on
the covers of* Good Housekeeping
magazine.

1, 2 *BOOK:* MOTHER GOOSE
DATE: 1914

4 *BOOK:* THE WATER BABIES
by Charles Kingsley
DATE: 1911

5 *BOOK:* THE EVERYDAY FAIRY
BOOK
DATE: 1917

1

2

3

4

5

*Born in Edinburgh, Scotland.
Trained at Heatherley's
Art School in London and
subsequently joined the staff
of* The Illustrated London
News, *where he remained
until 1907. Books illustrated
include* The Song of Solomon
(1909), The Imitation of Christ
(1908), Joseph Conrad's The
Duel *(1905), Chaucer's* The
Canterbury Tales *(1913) and
Malory's* Le Morte D'Arthur
*(1911). Magazine clients
included* Tatler, The English
Illustrated Magazine, Black
& White, The Idler *and* The
Sketch. *From the 1920s, Flint
made his name as a technically
brilliant water colourist,
specializing in scenes featuring
sensual semi- nude nymphets
in idealized landscapes. These,
and his colour illustrations for
lavishly produced gift books,
published by the Medici Society,
were enthusiastically acclaimed
by the public. He was elected
Royal Academician in 1933 and
was knighted in 1947.*

1

1 *BOOK:* LE MORTE D'ARTHUR
by Thomas Malory
DATE: 1911

2 *BOOK:* THE HEROES *by
Charles Kingsley*
DATE: 1912

2

1

2

*Born in New York. He started
drawing as a child and by
the age of 14 was already
financially independent of
his family through selling his
drawings. At 14 he sold his first
illustration to* Life *magazine,
and subsequently became a
member of its staff. At 16 he
studied at the Art Students
League in New York and at
20 he spent a year in England
where he illustrated his first
book,* Yankee Girls Abroad.
Magazine clients included
Judge, Life, Good Housekeeping,
Cosmopolitan, Liberty *and*
Harper's Weekly. *From 1903 he
drew portraits of the Hollywood
stars for* Photoplay *magazine
and these were later collated
in a book called* Celebrities
(1951). Other books include
City People *(1909) and* The
Adventures of Kitty Cobb *(1912).
Flagg designed 46 posters for
the war effort during World War
I, including the "I Want You"
image for* Leslie's Weekly. *During
World War II, his "Uncle Sam"
posters re-emerged and could be
found outside recruiting stations
across America.*

1 *POSTER:* U.S. MARINES
DATE: c. 1914

2 *POSTER:* U.S. ARMY
DATE: c. 1914

3 *MAGAZINE:* COSMOPOLITAN
DATE: 1918

4 *MAGAZINE:* COSMOPOLITAN
DATE: 1918

3   4

Illustrator, graphic designer and poster designer. His work tended to rely on strong, simple imagery and flat colours, and was perfectly suited to the style that emerged from the development of the London Underground and LNER railway posters in the 1930s. In 1926 he wrote and illustrated a book, Training in Commercial Art, which covered every aspect of the subject. In his instructions on the subject of travel posters he reveals the underlying principles of his own work: "It is not easy to render trees, grass-lands, water etc. in broad, flat treatment. Make careful studies of the different formations and shapes of trees, shrubs etc. Whenever possible avoid putting in clouds. Clear skies indicate fine weather and clear atmosphere." His work was prolific and he was a champion of the belief that the aesthetic statements of commercial art were as important and as valid as those found in fine art.

1

2

1 ADVERTISEMENT: SHELL
DATE: 1926

2 POSTER: LNER
DATE: 1920

3 POSTER: LNER
DATE: 1924

3

1

*Born in Ringwood, UK. Studied
at Birmingham School of Art
and in France and Italy. He
lived in the USA between 1915
and 1922, and lectured on
design and stage decoration at
the Universities of Columbia,
California and New Mexico, and
published a number of books
on technique. He was also a
painter, etcher, poet, composer
and writer. Books illustrated
include his own* The Hanging
Garden *(1914), Andersen's* The
Ugly Duckling and Other Tales
(1913), Armfield's Animal Book
(1922) and Shakespeare's The
Winter's Tale. *Armfield was a
leading member of the Tempera
Society, and his decorative
works, executed with care and
refinement, were influenced by
early Renaissance painting.*

1, 2 *BOOK:* ARMFIELD'S
ANIMAL BOOK
DATE: 1922

3, 4 *BOOK:* HANS ANDERSEN'S
TALES
DATE: 1910

2

3

4

LEONETTO CAPIELLO
(1875-1942)

*Born at Livorno, Italy. After
studies in his native town, he
settled in Paris to work as a
poster artist and illustrator. He
published a book of caricatures
(1896) and contributed to* Le
Rive, Le Journal, Le Figaro *and*
Le Gaulois. *His theatre and
advertising posters – such
as "Folies-Betgère" (1900),
"Cinzano" (1910) and "Le P'tit
Jeune Homme" (for the play
"Polaire", 1910) – show his
mastery of line and rhythm,
and he held to the importance of
these elements, believing colour
to be a secondary factor in the
success of a design. In reducing
the graphic elaboration that had
been a feature of earlier poster
work, Capiello moved towards
the modern interpretation of the
poster as an instantly attractive
and memorable image..*

1

2

1 ADVERTISEMENT: REVEL
UMBRELLAS
DATE: 1922

2 ADVERTISEMENT:
THERMOGENE
DATE: 1909

3 ADVERTISEMENT: CAMPARI
CORDIAL
DATE: 1921

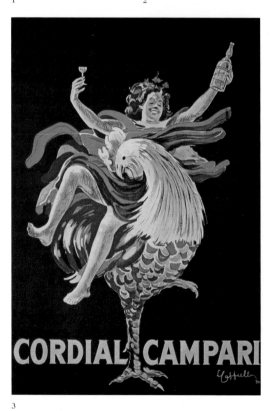

3

1   2

Born in Dublin, Ireland, the son of a stained glass artist. Studied at Dublin Metropolitan School of Art, where he won a travelling scholarship in 1914 to study early stained glass in the Ile-de-France. Clarke was one of the most successful followers of Beardsley, his imagery encompassing a powerful blend of horror, drama and humour. He is remembered today both for the beauty of his illustrations for the fairy tales of Hans Andersen and Charles Perrault and for the power and invention of his horror-fantasy style, which has influenced many fantasy and science fiction artists since.

His illustrations for Edgar Allan Poe's Tales of Mystery and Imagination *(1919) and Goethe's* Faust *(1925) moved an art critic, writing in* The Studio *in 1923, to write: "Never before have these marvellous tales been visually interpreted with such flesh-creeping, brain-taunting illusions of horror, terror and the unspeakable." Clarke was also a talented designer of stained glass and won the only gold medals awarded for stained glass at the Kensington Exhibitions in 1911, 1912 and 1913. He died of tuberculosis at the age of 42.*

1 *BOOK:* THE YEARS AT THE SPRING
DATE: 1920

2, 3 *BOOK:* TALES OF MYSTERY AND IMAGINATION *by Edgar Allan Poe*
DATE: 1919

3

1

2

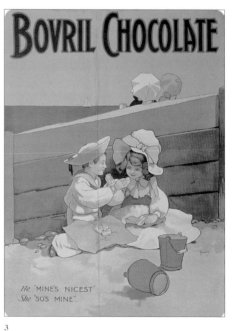

3

"PLEASE WILL YOU CLEAN FIDO ?"

4

5

6

Born in Walmer, UK, and educated in Devon and Heidelberg, Germany. After a brief spell as a farmer in Manitoba, Canada, he took up art, and had drawings accepted by The Graphic *and* Punch. *After studying art in Antwerp and Paris, he returned to England in 1895, where he became a successful cartoonist and advertising artist, designing some of the most effective posters of his day, including the well-known "Skegness Is So Bracing"(1908). He was granted a civil pension by George VI for his services to poster art. Hassall began illustrating children's books in the late 1890s, using the bold outlines and flat colour washes that characterised his posters. He also illustrated* John Hassall's New Picture Book *(1908),* Keep Smiling *(1916) and* Ye Berlyn Tapestrie *(1916), and contributed to* The Daily Sketch, Illustrated Bits, The Graphic, The Idler *and* The West End Review.

1 *POSTER:* THE ARRIVAL OF
PETER PAN
DATE: c. 1920

2 *TRAVEL POSTER:* NORTH
AFRICAN MOTOR TOURS
DATE: c. 1922

3 *ADVERTISEMENT:* BOVRIL
CHOCOLATE
DATE: c. 1920

4 *ADVERTISEMENT:* EASTMAN'S
CLEANING
DATE: c. 1900

5 *ADVERTISEMENT:* HMV
GRAMOPHONES
DATE: c. 1915

6 *BOOK:* NURSERY RHYMES
ILLUSTRATED
DATE: c. 1910

Born in Zurich, Switzerland. Apprenticed to a lithographer, then went onto study at the Konigliche Akademie in Munich, and also in Paris and London. In 1920 he worked on stage designs for productions in Berlin and Zurich, and in the same year began to teach lithography and life drawing at the School of Arts and Crafts in Zurich. Commercial work of the 1920s typically included "super-real" lithography images advertising clothing products – coats, hats, shoes – but he also produced highly graphic information posters constructed of geometric shapes and typography. During the 1930s he developed a looser, almost painterly style. His career demonstrated a range of design interests, from illustration and advertising design to stage design and mural painting.

1 ADVERTISEMENT: PKZ
DATE: 1922

2 ADVERTISEMENT: FACO
FLOOR COVERINGS
DATE: c. 1919

3 ADVERTISEMENT:
DOSENBACH'S SHOE MARKET
DATE: c. 1919

4 ADVERTISEMENT: WECK
DATE: c. 1919

1

2

3

4

1

2

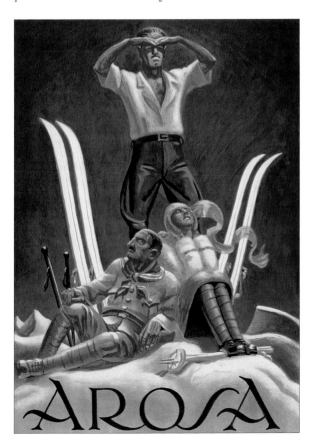

3

Born in Zurich. During his lifetime Bickel worked as an illustrator, painter, sculptor and graphic artist. From 1900-04 he was an apprentice lithographer and then spent four years in a Zurich advertising agency while taking evening classes at the School of Arts and Crafts, where he studied under E Stiefel. In 1908 he started his own advertising agency and continued his studies until he moved to Italy in 1912. He spent a year there and was strongly influenced by the works of Michelangelo and Leonardo da Vinci. On his return to Switzerland he made his first attempts at sculpture and from 1914-17 concentrated on portraiture, etching and landscape painting. From 1917 until his death he was primarily a commercial artist, designing and illustrating stamps, posters and murals.

1 *ADVERTISEMENT:*
SCHEURERSHOES
DATE: 1920

2 *ADVERTISEMENT:* MAZZANTI
LIGHTING
DATE: 1915

3 *TRAVEL POSTER:* AROSA
DATE: 1927

JEAN DEBOSSCHERE
(1878-1953)

Born in Uccle, Belgium. Studied at the Beaux Arts d'Anvers. After working in Paris, Brussels, London and Italy, he finally settled at Fontainebleau, near Paris, in 1929 (he became a French citizen in 1959). His work was wide-ranging as writer, illustrator, designer, printer and book collector. His first book as author and illustrator was Béale-Gyne (1909): his own books included The City Curious *(1920) and* Job le Pauvre *(1923), and* Gulliver's Travels *(1920) and* Don Quixote *(1922) were among the classic titles that he illustrated. He also contributed to* The Little Review, The Monthly Chapbook, The New Coterie, *and* Reveille. *In his Beardsleyesque images, with solid blacks set against rhythmic lines, the characterization sometimes has a hint of the surreal.*

1, 2 *BOOK:* THE POEMS OF
OSCAR WILDE
DATE: 1927

3, 4 *BOOK:* THE CITY CURIOUS
DATE: 1920

1

2

3

4

1

2

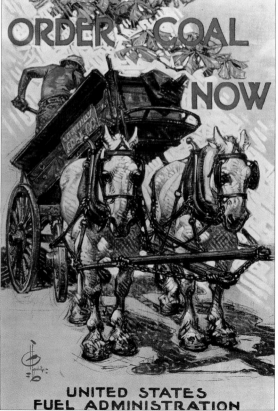

3

*Born in Montabour, Germany.
In 1882 he moved with his
parents to Chicago, USA and
at age 16 was apprenticed
to an engraving company, at
the same time taking evening
classes at the Chicago Art
Institute. In 1896 he won first
prize in* The Century *magazine's
competition to illustrate one of
their covers (Maxfield Parrish
came second) and he and his
younger brother studied at
the Academic Julien in Paris
for two years before returning
to the USA to set up their
own studio. His illustrations
appeared in magazines such
as* Collier's, Success, Up to
Date *and* The Saturday Evening
Post. *He also illustrated war
bond posters (during World
War II) and advertisements
for Kellogg's cornflakes, Ivory
soap, Chesterfield cigarettes and
Arrow collars and shirts. He
originated the Arrow Shirt collar
man, which became the epitome
of elegant style sought after by
the public.*

1 *MAGAZINE:* THE SATURDAY
EVENING POST
DATE: PUBLISHED 1940

2 *ADVERTISEMENT:* ARROW
COLLARS
DATE: 1913

3 *POSTER*
DATE: c. 1916

1

2

3

4

5

6

*Born in London. Studied at the
Regent Street and Heatherley
Art Schools. From 1911 until
the end of her life, Attwell's
work appeared in annuals and
gift books and on countless
advertisements, posters,
calendars, wall plaques
and greetings cards, which
she designed for Valentine
of Dundee. Her chubby,
mischievous toddlers, often
featured in situations with
adult overtones, conveyed a
sentimental and nostalgic view
of daily life between the wars.
During the first decades of
the century Attwell illustrated
such fairy-tale classics as*
Mother Goose *(1910),* Alice in
Wonderland *(1911) and* Hans
Andersen's Fairy Tales *(1914),
as well as Charles Kingsley's*
The Water Babies *(1915) and J
M Barrie's* Peter Pan and Wendy
*(1921). She also contributed
to* The Tatler, The Bystander,
Graphic *and* The Illustrated
London News.

1, 5, 6 *BOOK:* PETER PAN AND
WENDY *by J M Barrie*
DATE: 1921

2 *GREETINGS CARD*
DATE: c. 1920

3 *ADVERTISEMENT:* VIM
CLEANING POWDER
DATE: c. 1910

4 *POSTER:* "WHERE DO FLIES
GO IN WINTER-TIME?"
DATE: c. 1915

ROBERT GIBBINGS
(1889-1958)

Born in Cork, Ireland. His parents wanted him to be a doctor but, after failing at medical school he was eventually allowed to attend the Slade School of Art in London. His career was then stalled by World War I, during which he served at Gallipoli and it was not until 1918 that he became a freelance artist, specializing in wood engraving. His early work tended to the simplicity of silhouettes, but in time he developed an extraordinarily precise technique that brought a great richness of detail to his engravings. In 1924 he bought the Golden Cockerel Press and set up as a printer of fine editions. He sold it in 1933 and lectured on book production at Heading University until 1942, when he left to concentrate on his own work and to travel. In all he illustrated 61 books and was the author of 14, including Lovely is the Lee *(1945),* Coming Down the Wye *(1952),* Sweet Cork of Thee *(1951),* Coming Down the Seine *(1953) and* Trumpets from Montparnasse *(1955). His last work,* Till I End My Song, *was published in 1957, a year before his death.*

1

2

3

1 *BOOK:* THE GIRL IN THE GARRET *by Robert Gibbings*
DATE: 1921

2 *POSTER:* LONDON TRANSPORT
DATE: 1922

3 *WOOD ENGRAVING:* "FOWEY HARBOUR"
DATE: 1921

4 *WOOD ENGRAVING:* "CHELSEA BRIDGE"
DATE: 1921

4

1

3

Born in Munich, Germany, son
of the portrait painter Franz
Moos. In 1897 he began his
career as an illustrator for a
Munich daily newspaper. In
1915 he established himself in
Munich, where he divided his
time between painting mountain
landscapes and working for a
local design group. His excellent
draughtsmanship, combined
with gentle but graphic use of
colour, ensured his success both
as an illustrator of posters and
as a scenic artist.

1 POSTER: "VOTE FOR
FREEDOM OF THE SPIRIT"
DATE: 1935

2 ADVERTISEMENT: CAFFE
HAG
DATE: 1927

3 TRAVEL POSTER: ST MORITZ
DATE: 1929

2

GEORGE STUDDY
(1878-1948)

Born in Devon, UK. Studdy developed a childhood interest in drawing while confined to a hospital bed and later contributed his work to boys' magazines while a student at Dulwich College. On graduating from Heatherley's School of Art he worked as an engineer's draughtsman until 1906, when, after seeing the Royal Academy Summer Show, he was inspired to become a humorous artist. He illustrated regularly for The Sketch *magazine, where he developed the character of "Bonzo", the mischievous puppy which made him famous and which appeared on postcards, jigsaw puzzles and posters. In fact Bonzo became so popular that he escaped the confines of the media normally available to illustrators and appeared on ashtrays, car mascots, sweets, cigarette cards and other ephemera, all of which have become collectable items today. He also appeared in books and annuals and became a star of stage and screen. This craze peaked in the 1920s and Bonzo's popularity declined after Studdy's death from lung cancer in 1948.*

1, 2 *BOOK:* A BOX OF TRICKS
DATE: 1922

3, 4 *BOOK:* PUPPY TAILS
DATE: 1922

1

2

3

4

1

Born in Wolstanton, UK. Studied at Burslem School of Art, the Royal College of Art, and in Italy. The range of his work included painting, book illustration and ceramic and stained glass design. From 1935-38 he held the post of Principal at the Regent Street Polytechnic School of Art in London. As an illustrator he is known for work on children's books, such as Charles Kingsley's The Water Babies (1922), Stories of King Arthur (1925) and Grimm's Fairy Tales (1930), and he contributed to the periodical Holly Leaves. His skill as a water colourist is reflected in the pleasing colouring of his illustrative work.

1, 2 *BOOK:* GULLIVER'S TRAVELS *by Jonathan Swift DATE: 1920*

3 *BOOK:* GRIMM'S FAIRY TALES *DATE: 1930*

2

3

1

2

3

Born in London. Studied at Heatherky's and the Slade Art Schools and at Frank Calderori's School of Animal Painting. From 1896-1902 he was chief artist at the magazine publishers Arthur Pearson Ltd, during which time he gained valuable practical experience in commercial work and learned about the printing process so that he could best ensure the quality of his published drawings. During his career he became very popular with the public for his witty and technically brilliant illustrations of animals and people and contributed to Graphic, The Illustrated London News and Punch. He also illustrated a number of books, including Old Nursery Rhymes (1931), Lawson Wood's Fun Fair (1931) and his famous series The Merry Monkeys (1946). He was a close friend of Tom Browne and a fellow member of the London Sketch Club.

1 POSTCARD
DATE: 1906

2 POSTCARD
DATE: 1906

3, 4 BOOK: THE MERRY MONKEYS by Arthur Groom
DATE: 1946

5 BOOK: BRUSH, PEN AND PENCIL by A E Johnson
DATE: 1910

4

5

FRED TAYLOR
(1875-1963)

Born in London. Studied at the Académie Julien in Paris, Goldsmith's College School of Art in London, and in Italy. An accomplished landscape and architectural painter, he was one of the artists commissioned for poster work by London Midland & Scottish Railways and London Underground during the 1920s and 1930s. Images such as "The Heart of the Empire", an aerial view of Westminster and the Houses of Parliament, "Trafalgar Square", and "Chigwell", a graphic view of a Tudor-style inn, show Taylor's superb grasp of architectural structure and detail and a subtle approach to colour, while "Hampstead Fair" describes the holiday crowd enjoying the fair in a riot of bold bright hues. His control of line in black-and-white rendering is equally crisp and immediate.

1

1 *POSTER:* ENSIGNETTE
DATE: c. 1915

2 *POSTER:* LONDON
UNDERGROUND
DATE: 1920

3 *POSTER:* LONDON & NORTH
EASTERN RAILWAY
DATE: c. 1923

2

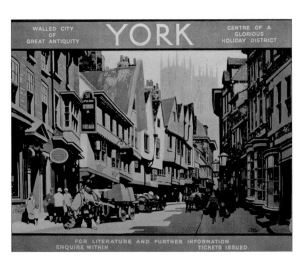

3

1

Born in Needham, USA. Wyeth was a devotee of his teacher, Howard Pyle, and depicted similar subjects – medieval life, Americana and pirates – and captured dramatic scenes in rich decorative colours. He was extremely prolific and during his lifetime produced more than 3,000 illustrations, murals, still lifes and landscape paintings. Among them were more than 25 books for Charles Scribner's Sons' Classic Series, including J Boyd's Drums *(1928), Stevenson's* David Balfour *(1924) and J F Cooper's* The Deerslayer *(1925), some of which are still in print today. One of the finest examples of his work is J F Coopers* Last of the Mohicans *(1919). He was an extremely popular figure in America, and his skills were inherited by his extraordinarily talented family – most notable being his son Andrew.*

1, 2 *BOOK:* ROBIN HOOD
DATE: 1921

3 *PAINTING:* "INDIAN BRAVE
FISHING"
DATE: c. 1900

2

3

1

2

3

4

5

A M CASSANDRE
(1901-1968)

*Born Adolphe Mouran in Russia.
Studied at the Académie Julien
in Paris. From 1922-28 he
designed posters for Hachard
and Co, and in 1930 he founded
the Alliance Graphique with
Charles Loupot and Maurice
Moyrand. Influenced by Léger,
Delaunay and the Italian
Futurists, he took elements
from avant-garde painting and
design and popularized them
in his brilliant posters, widely
acknowledged as among the
best to have come out of France
during the 1930s. His designs for
the French National Railways,
and those for the ocean liners
L'Atlantique (1931) and
Normandie (1935), are classics
of their genre. He also designed
theatre sets and costumes,
typefaces for Olivetti, and ran
a small art school where André
François was one of his pupils.*

1 *POSTER:* BELGIAN RAILWAYS
DATE: 1929

2 *POSTER:* LONDON, MIDLAND
SCOTTISH RAILWAY
DATE: 1928

3 *POSTER:* FRENCH NORTHERN
RAILWAYS
DATE: 1929

4 *POSTER:* BELGIAN RAILWAYS
DATE: 1927

5 *POSTER:* FRENCH
TRANSATLANTIC LINE
DATE: 1935

Born in Szeged, Hungary. He started working while still a child, to help support his family after his father's death, and paid for his own education at the Budapest Technical School where he studied engineering by giving tuition to fellow students. He later attended the Academy of Art in Budapest and studied art in Paris and Munich. In 1906 he moved to London, where he became a protégé of Edmund Dulac (a fellow member of the London Sketch Club) and where he became a very successful illustrator. Books illustrated include The Rime of the Ancient Mariner (1910), The Rubaiyat of Omar Khayyam (1909) and Goethe's Faust (1912). In 1915 he settled in New York, where he continued to illustrate books and also designed hotel interiors and stage sets. He worked in Hollywood as an art director for Warner Studios until the 1930s. Poga y's best illustrations were in pen and ink, a medium in which he was remarkably fluent.

1

1 *MAGAZINE*: LEJOURNAL DE
LA DECORATION
DATE: c. 1900

2 ORIENTAL MOTIFS NO 4
DATE: c. 1900

3 ORIENTAL MOTIFS NO 3
DATE: c. 1900

4 *BOOK*: LEGENDS OF THE
MIDDLE AGES
DATE: 1914

5, 6 *BOOK*: NURSERY RHYMES
DATE: 1919

7 *BOOK*: GULLIVER'S TRAVELS
by *Jonathan Swift*
DATE: 1919

2   3

4

5

6

7

EDMUND SULLIVAN
(1869-1933)

*Born in London. His father was
an artist and Sullivan studied
under him until the age of
20, when he joined* The Daily
Graphic. *Although perhaps
overshadowed by Dulac and
Rackham, he quickly established
himself as a fine draughtsman
with two distinct styles – black-
and-white work in pen and ink
and a looser, gentler treatment
with washes and chalk lines.
He was a devotee of Phil May
and in his own words, wanted
to express "the character
the solid body is possessed
of – the spiritual essence ...
and the impact made on the
whole complex mind and not
only upon, or by, the retina".
He contributed to many of the
publications of his day and
illustrated nearly 20 books,
including Wells'* Modern Utopia
(1905), The Pilgrim's Progress
(1901) and The Rubaiyat of
Omar Khayyam *(1913). He
was also highly influential as a
teacher, lecturing at Goldsmith's
College of Art and producing a
detailed instruction manual* The
Art of Illustration *(1921).*

1 *BOOK:* DREAM OF FAIR
WOMEN *by Alfred Tennyson
DATE:* 1900

2 *ADVERTISEMENT:* SHELL
FUELS
DATE: 1923

1

2

1

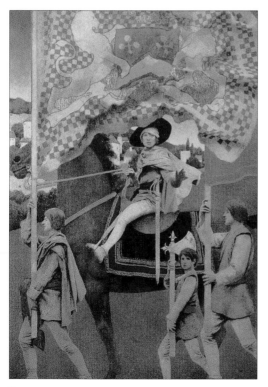

2

3

Born in Philadelphia, USA. Educated at Haverford College, the Pennsylvania Academy of Fine Arts, and studied under Howard Pyle at the Drexel Institute. He illustrated for a number of magazines, including Harper's Weekly, Collier's *and* Time. *Books illustrated include* Dream Days *(1906) by kenneth Grahame,* Poems of Childhood *(1889) by Eugene Field and The* Knave of Hearts *(1925) by Louise Saunders. His unique combination of colour, exotic characters and fanciful settings won him much popular acclaim during his lifetime.*

1 *ADVERTISEMENT:*
JELL-ODESSERT
DATE: 1924

2 *BOOK:* THE KING ALBERT
BOOK
DATE: 1914

3 *MAGAZINE:* THE CENTURY
DATE: c. 1930

ERIC GILL
(1882-1940)

Born in Brighton, UK. Studied at Chichester Art School and the Central School of Arts and Crafts in London. He began his career as a letter-cutter and sign writer, then turned to figure carving in wood and stone. In 1913 he became a Catholic and, after World War 1, formed the Guild of St Joseph and St Dominic – a society of craftsmen dedicated to reviving a religious attitude towards art and craft. A versatile artist, he was a very skilful engraver, illustrating many books for Robert Gibbings at the Golden Cockerel Press from 1924. He was also a sculptor of international repute and played an enormous part in the development of English 20th-century typography.

1 *BOOK:* THE FOUR GOSPELS
DATE: 1931

2 *BOOK:* PASSIO DOMINI
NOSTRI JESUCHRISTI
DATE: 1926

3 *BOOKJACKET:* THE ALDINE
BIBLE
DATE: 1934

1

2

3

1

Born in Sheffield, UK. Studied at the Academy of Art in Dusseldorf, where he was a rebellious student, and was expelled in 1884. He returned to England before continuing his studies in Antwerp and Paris, where French poster art had a lasting influence on his own work. His most famous poster are "The Gaiety Girl", for Sir Augustus Harris's theatrical venture, and "The Yellow Girl" which advertised Jerome K Jerome's new publication Today. The later was particularly popular and started a craze for posters in England.

1 *PROGRAMME DESIGN:*
BERTRAM MILLS' CIRCUS
DATE: 1921

CHARLES PAINE
(1873-1964)

*Born in Queenstown,
Pennsylvania, USA. In 1886 he
drew cartoons for the* Pittsburgh
Post, *using the trademark of a
little racoon. Over the next few
years he created other strips,
including* Coon Hollow Folks,
Bear Creek Folks *and* Scary
William, *for newspapers in
Pittsburgh and Philadelphia.
Paine had a very individual and
decorative style, with sketchy,
boldly coloured figures drawn
inside circles, rather than the
usual panel format. When he
became successful he moved to
California, from where he sent*
Honeybunch's Hubby *to New
York for publication three times
a week. However, his fame rests
on his classic strip* S'Matter
Pop? *featuring the adventures
of Pop, Willyum and Desperate
Ambrose. It was first published
in* World *in 1917 and ran for 30
years. After its demise, Paine
fell into obscurity and died
penniless in New York.*

1

1 *ADVERTISEMENT;* SHELL OIL
DATE: 1928

---

2 *POSTER:* LONDON
TRANSPORT
DATE: 1922

---

3 *PUBLICITY POSTER:* WELWYN
GARDEN CITY
DATE: 1939

2

3

1

2

*Born Käthe Schmidt in
Konigsberg Germany. Studied
painting in Munich, where
she discovered what was to
become a life-long preference
for black-and-white media.
She married a doctor and lived
in the poor northern sector
of Berlin, where her husband
worked and where she took up
etching. Sharing with Gauguin
the belief that "ugliness can be
beautiful, prettiness never", her
art was an expression of her
solidarity with the oppressed
and poverty-stricken. In the
late 1890s she achieved fame
as a socialist artist with her
illustrations for Hauptmann's*
The Weavers' Uprising, *and in
1902 she was much praised for
her series* The Peasants' War, *In
1909 she contributed drawings
to the satirical magazine*
Simplizissimus *and the following
year took up sculpture. In 1919
she began producing woodcuts,
a medium whose bold simplicity
was well suited to her subjects
and themes. Her son was
killed in World War I and she
remained passionately opposed
to war, producing "The War"
series of woodcuts in 1923.*

1 *ETCHING:* "PEASANTS' WAR"
DATE: 1903

2 *ETCHING:* "PEASANTS' WAR"
DATE: 1907

EDWARD PENFIELD
(1866-1925)

Illustrator, poster artist and writer, born in the USA. While Lautrec, Mucha and Chéret were enjoying the "Golden Age of the Poster" in Europe, Penfield was producing some of the best poster work in America. His style was to draw in silhouetted shapes that had been refined from careful preliminary sketches. The effect was deceptive, in that when seen from a distance the simplicity of the treatment made the subject immediately recognizable and yet when seen in close-up the work contained sufficient detail to hold the viewer's interest. In the first two decades of the century his work appeared frequently on the covers of magazines such as Collier's *and he illustrated many calendars, the most notable being his redrawing of the* Old Farmer's Almanac *for the Beck Engraving Company in 1918. He also wrote and illustrated the outstanding* Holland Sketches, *which was published by* Scribner's *in 1907. Penfield had a lasting influence on American illustration through his work, his teaching at the Art Students League and his years as art director of* Harper's *magazine. He was president of the Society of Illustrators in 1921 and 1922.*

---

1 *BOOK:* THREE GRINGOS IN CENTRAL AMERICA AND VENEZUELA *by Richard Harding*
DATE: c. 1900

2 *PUBLICITY POSTER:* HARPER'S MAGAZINE
DATE: c. 1900

3 *ADVERTISEMENT:* HART SCHAFFNER & MARX OUTFITTERS
DATE: NOT KNOWN

1

2

3

1

2

3

*Born in Malta. Studied
at Lambeth School of Art.
He developed a humorous
style with heavy outlines
that was reminiscent of his
contemporaries, John Hassall
and Tom Browne. His work was
very popular and he contributed
frequently to magazines such
as* Punch, The Sketch, Tatler,
The Strand Magazine, The
Graphic, The Idler *and the*
Humorist. *He developed a
working relationship with the
humorous writer WW Jacobs
and illustrated four of his books,
including* Sailor's Knots *(1909)
and* Short Cruises *(1920). He
also wrote and illustrated five
books of his own –* Alleged
Humour *(1917),* Three Jolly
Sailors and Me *(1919),* Old
London Town *(1921),* Mr
Peppercorn *(1940) and* What's
The Dope? *(1944). However, his
style was best suited to posters
and he produced a great many
for such clients as Lux washing
powders and Sunlight soap.*

1 *ADVERTISEMENT:* LUX SOAP
FLAKES
DATE: c. 1920

2 *ADVERTISEMENT:* SUNLIGHT
SOAP
DATE: c. 1920

3 *PUBLICITY POSTER*
DATE: c. 1920

Grew up and was schooled in France. The son of a portrait painter, Rooke studied at the Slade in London from 1899-1903 and then under Edward Johnstone at the Central School of Art, where Eric Gill was one of his contemporaries. In 1904 he took up wood engraving. He drew directly on to the wood block working in both black and white line, and experimented with graduated tones and wood-cutting. Although he was familiar with the techniques of colour printing he mostly limited himself to black and white in his book illustrations.

1 *POSTER:* LONDON
TRANSPORT
DATE: c. 1900

2 *POSTER:* LONDON
TRAMWAYS
DATE: c. 1900

3 *POSTER:* LONDON
TRAMWAYS
DATE: c. 1900

1

2

3

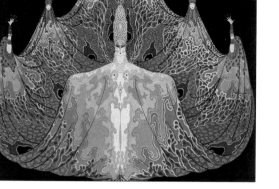

1

Born in St Petersburg
(Leningrad), Russia. Moving
to Paris in 1912, be became
a designer with the couturier
Paul Poiret. He adopted the
pseudonym Erté from the French
pronunciation of his initials, R T
(Remain de Tirtoff). He designed
magazine covers and fashion
plates for Harper's Bazaar over
a period of more than 20 years,
although he also contributed to
Vogue and others. Erté's designs
were typically elaborate and
stylish. His illustrations, in
black and white or vivid colour,
ranged from richly decorative
Art Deco fantasies to fluidly
elegant, practical modern
clothing and he was frequently
able to combine a graphic visual
economy with careful attention
to descriptive detail.

1 COSTUME DESIGN
DATE: c. 1920

2 COSTUME DESIGN
DATE: 1921

2

*Born Georg Ehrenfiied Gro
in Germany. Studied at the
Dresden Academy of Art
and had his first satirical
drawings published in the
comic magazine* Ulk *at the
age of 17. He also studied in
Paris and at the Berlin School
of Arts and Crafts, where he
made a living by selling his
caricatures. By 1919 he was a
leading member of the Dada art
movement in Berlin, and, with
John Heartfield edited satirical
magazines of the political left
which made him unpopular
with the Nazis. An opponent
of what he called "the slavish
copying of nature", he believed
in the expressive use of line. At
his most brilliant in* Ecce Homo
*(1923), which was confiscated
by the police and led to an
indecency trial Grosz's harsh
images and startling use of line
and colour perfectly express
his contempt for the decadent
bourgeoisie. His illustrations
have had an enormous influence
on subsequent generations of
artists and illustrators. In 1932
he moved to New York where
he taught at the Art Students
League*

1-7 *BOOK:* ECCE HOMO
DATE: 1923

1

2

3

4

5

6

7

*Born in New York. His early
talent for drawing was
encouraged, and he studied at
the Mark Hopkins Institute of
Art in San Francisco. At the age
of 16, and while still a student,
his work was published in
the local newspapers. After
leaving college he returned to
New York and worked as a
staff artist on Puck. By now his
talent for drawing women was
established; his Fisher Body Girl
was a trade mark for years and
led to an exclusive contract to
illustrate the monthly covers for*
Cosmopolitan *magazine, which
he did for several years.*

1 *MAGAZINE:* COSMOPOLITAN
DATE: 1920

2 *MAGAZINE:* COSMOPOLITAN
DATE: 1920

3 *MAGAZINE:* COSMOPOLITAN
DATE: 1920

4 *MAGAZINE:* COSMOPOLITAN
DATE: 1920

1

2

3

4

1

*Born in Ohio, USA. Studied
at the Art Students League
and the National Academy in
New York and was taken on
by William Merritt Chase as a
private student at his famous
10th Street Studio. Initially
Christy planned to be a fine
artist, but after selling his
work to Scribner's, Harper's
and Leslie's Weekly he chose
a more commercial career.
During the Spanish-American
conflict he worked as a War
Artist and went with the US
troops to Cuba. However, he
is remembered mostly for
his drawings of women. His
subjects were usually healthy,
outdoor types who became
known as the "Christy Girls",
and were popular with the
public and with magazine
publishers.*

1 *MAGAZINE:* COSMOPOLITAN
DATE: 1918

ANNE ANDERSON
(1874-1930)

Born in Scotland, but spent her childhood in Argentina before finally settling in England. She worked on over 100 children s books, including treasuries and annuals, sometimes in collaboration with her husband Alan Wright. She produced several titles as both author and illustrator, among them The Funny Bunny ABC *(1912),* The Cosy Corner Book *(1943), and* The Podgy Puppy *(1927). Her decorative line work and delicate colouring showed the influence of Art Nouveau and also owed something to the style of Mabel Lucie Attwell. Her illustrations were particularly popular during the 1920s and she also produced greetings card designs. Her work has proved enduringly popular and her illustrated* Grimm's Fairy Tales *(1928 and 1929) have been reprinted many times.*

1 *CHRISTMAS CARD*
DATE: c. 1930

2 *BOOK:* OLD ENGLISH
NURSERY SONGS
DATE: NOTKNOWN

3 *BOOK:* THE GOLDEN
WONDER BOOK
DATE: 1934

4 *BOOK:* OLD ENGLISH
NURSERY SONGS
DATE: NOT KNOWN

1

2

3

4

1

2

3

4

JEAN DE BRUNHOFF
(1899-1937)

Born in Paris. Studied under Othon Friesz. De Brunhoff will always be remembered for his stories and illustrations of Babar the Elephant, a character he created for the amusement of his children. The simple water colour drawings were accompanied by text in clear but child-like handwriting. The first book, The Story of Babar, *was published in Paris in 1931 and soon after in London and New York, and was an immediate success.* Babar's Travels *and* Babar the King *soon followed, and the stories of Babar and the inhabitants of the town of Celesteville were serialized in* The Daily Sketch *in the UK. In 1936 the books were translated into eight languages, making Babar the internationally famous character that he remains to this day. De Brunhoff died at the age of 38 and the last two books,* Babar and Family *(1938) and* Babar and Father Christmas *(1939), were completed by his brother Michel and son Laurent. In 1988 Babar reached the big screen in* The Babar Story, *an English-speaking animated feature directed by Alan Bunce.*

1-3 *BOOK:* BABAR THE KING
by Jean de Brunhoff
DATE: 1938

4 *BOOK:* BABAR AND FATHER
CHRISTMAS *by Jean de Brunhoff*
DATE: c. 1939

*Born in New South Wales,
Australia. His family returned
to England when he was a
child and he studied at the
Westminster and New Cross
Art Schools, after which he
worked in the studio of Charles
Van Havenmaet for several
years. In 1906, encouraged by
Phil May (a fellow member of
the London Sketch Club), he
began contributing humorous
drawings to* Tatler, Scraps,
Punch *and* The Graphic.
*After 1911, he revolutionized
humorous art in Britain with
his* The Man Who... *series of
cartoons, which exploited
middle-class mores and the
fear of committing a faux pas.
His barking colonels, haughty
matriarchs and timid little men
were drawn from his own social
milieu, and the comic situations
focused on the social arenas of
the party, the club, and the meal
table. Books include* Bateman's
Booklets *(1931),* The Art of
the Caricature *(1936) and* H M
Bateman by Himself *(1937). He
also illustrated advertisements
for the London tailors Moss Bros,
Lucky Strike cigarettes and
Guinness beer, and designed
theatre posters.*

1 *WWII POSTER:* "UP AND AT'
EM!"
DATE: c. 1939

2 *BOOK:* BROUGHT FORWARD
DATE: 1932

3 *ADVERTISEMENT:* GUINNESS
BEER
DATE: 1937

1   2

3

1

*Born in Souris, Canada. His
family moved to Wales in 1896
and he studied at art schools in
Cardiff and Scotland continuing
evening studies after he moved
to London to begin his career.
After work in Canada as a
commercial artist, interrupted
by a period of service in Europe
during World War I, he settled
in London in 1922, where he
developed a strong and colourful
graphic style. Work for London
Transport posters, such as his
design for the Natural History
Museum in London (1928), led
to other similar commissions
from the Royal Mail shipping
company, BP Oil and many
others. In 1943 he began to
develop his painting skills
independently of commercial
work and became known as a
painter of abstracts.*

1 *ADVERTISEMENT:* BP OIL
DATE: 1933

2 *POSTER:* SOUTHERN
RAILWAY
DATE: 1930

3 *POSTER:* VICTORIA AND
ALBERT MUSEUM
DATE: 1934

2

3

ROCKWELL KENT
(1882-1971)

Born in New York. Trained as an architect but later studied art in New York with Robert Henri, Abbott Thayer and William Chase. He was one of a breed of American illustrators who combined artistic endeavour with a life of adventure. He spent the winter of 1918 on Fox Island in Alaska and his diaries and drawings were the source material for his own publication, Wilderness *(1920). This experience was still evident ten years later in his portrayal of* Moby Dick *(1930). However, neither work is really typical of his style. His architect's precision is better represented in* Salamina *(1935) and his interest in Art Deco in* Candide *(1928). His achievements went beyond illustration and he became famous as an engraver, lithographer, mural painter, writer and lecturer. Throughout his life he remained a controversial left-wing activist. He was blacklisted during the McCarthy era, in response to which he later refused the title of National Academician.*

1- 3 *BOOKPLATES*
DATE: c. 1937

1

2

3

1

THE QUICK-STARTING PAIR **SHELL OIL & PETROL**

2

PULLS like **SHELL!**

3

SHELL
OIL & PETROL

FAVOURITES

4

*Born in Bristol, UK. Studied
at Camberwell School of Art
and after graduating worked
for six years in advertising
before deciding to set up his
own studio. He quickly became
successful as a poster artist and
from 1920-50 his prolific output
could be seen on billboards
and hoardings all over the UK.
His style was characterized
by the use of bold colours and
minimal detail and his many
clients included Dewar's whisky,
Bovril the LNER, Shell-Mex,
BP and Austin Reed. In 1935
he helped organise the "British
Art In Industry" exhibition at
the Royal Academy and from
1940-45 he was an Official War
Artist, attached to the Ministry
of Supply, where he produced
posters that boosted British
morale and encouraged material
economies.*

1 *ADVERTISEMENT:* AUSTIN
REED
DATE: c. 1930

2 *ADVERTISEMENT:* SHELL OIL
DATE: 1931

3 *ADVERTISEMENT:* SHELLOIL
DATE: 1930

4 *ADVERTISEMENT:* SHELL OIL
DATE: 1928

AUBREY HAMMOND
(1894-1940)

Born in Folkestone, UK. Studied at the London and Byam Shaw Schools of Art, then attended the Académie Julien in Paris. He worked a great deal in pen and ink, drawing caricatures very much in the style of the 20s, and also developed a strong graphic style with flat colours that was extremely effective on posters. He illustrated several books, including The Diary of Mr Niggs *(1922), Lewis Melville's* The London Scene *(1926) and Peter Traill's* Under the Cherry Tree *(1926). He also worked as a scenic artist and taught commercial and theatrical design at the Westminster School of Art.*

1 *POSTER:* LONDON TRANSPORT
DATE: 1923

2 *POSTCARD:* CHARLES LAUGHTON
DATE: 1928

3 *ADVERTISEMENT:* "232" GREY FLANNELS
DATE: c. 1928

1

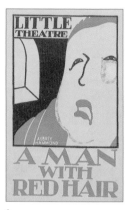

2

3

1

2

3

*Born in Eltham, UK. He was
an artistically gifted child
and studied for a year at the
Royal Academy Schools before
enrolling at the Slade School of
Fine Arts at the age of 17. Here
he was encouraged by Professor
Tonks and in 1926, when he was
just 21, he was commissioned
to paint a mural in the tea room
at the Tate Gallery. Inspired by
the Temple Gardens of Stowe
and Wilton, Whistler created
an architectural fantasy, called*
The Pursuit of Rare Meats *
that brought him immediate
recognition and success. One
of his earliest publications
was* Children of Hertha *(1929),
written by his brother Laurence,
Whistler went on to illustrate
three further books by his
brother,* Armed October *(1932),*
The Emperor Heart *(1936) and*
Oho *(1946). However, his classic
work is undoubtedly* Gulliver's
Travels *(1930), which contained
full-plate drawings in pen and
ink with colour washes applied
by hand. Whistler's work was
always witty, and during the
1930s he produced a Guinness
advertising campaign consisting
of faces drawn in pen and ink
which changed character when
viewed upside down. He also
designed for stage productions,
including* The Rake's Progress,
Victoria Regina, Fidelio *and* The
Marriage of Figaro.

1 *ADVERTISEMENT:* GUINNESS
BEER
DATE: c. 1937

2 *BOOK:* FAIRYTALES AND
LEGENDS *by Hans Christian
Andersen*
DATE: 1935

3 *POSTER:* SHELL FUELS
DATE: 1933

OTTO ERNST
1900-1939

Born in Kölliken, Switzerland. From 1906-07 he studied in Florence and Paris, where he was a student of E Grasset at the Académie de la Grande Chaumière He then returned to Switzerland where he exhibited his landscapes and lithographs and where his graphic style made him a successful designer and illustrator of posters.

1 *POSTER:* "WORLD CYCLE CHAMPIONSHIP"
DATE: 1923

2 *TRAVEL POSTER*
DATE: 1937

3 *TRAVEL POSTER*
DATE: 1930

1

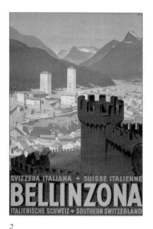

2

3

1

Born in Trieste, Italy. Educated in Bologna, where he later worked as a commercial artist. His mastery of line and use of strong colour and simple graphic designs made him a much sought after poster artist and he worked regularly for the Ricordi publishers in Milan and for advertising clients such as Gitane cigarettes in France. His work was exhibited in the Milan International Exhibition in 1905. He became a political caricaturist during the 1911 Tripoli War and was later a professor at the Brera Academy in Milan.

1 *ADVERTISING POSTER:*
SP1GA TYRES
DATE: 1931

2 *POSTER*
DATE: c. 1925

3 *POSTER*
DATE: c. 1920

4 *ADVERTISING POSTER:*
STREGALIQUEUR
DATE: 1911

2

3

4

Born in London. Studied etching and engraving at Goldsmith's College of Art. In 1932 he took up painting mainly semi-abstract landscapes of Wales, Cornwall and Pembrokeshire. An official War Artist during World War II, his illustrations of the devastation helped secure his developing reputation. From 1927-40 he taught at Kingston and Chelsea Schools of Art and designed stained glass and tableware decoration as well as illustrating for clients such as Jack Beddington at Shell. In 1942 he published his Pembrokeshire Sketchbook in Horizon magazine. He remains most famous for his paintings, which were influenced by Samuel Palmer. In the late 1940s he began to concentrate on portraiture and painted Somerset Maugham in 1949 and Winston Churchill in 1954. This latter portrait caused a controversy and was later destroyed by Churchill's family. In 1956 he moved to the South of France and the following year received his most famous commission, the Christ In Glory Tapestry at Coventry Cathedral.

1

2

1 POSTER: LONDON
TRANSPORT
DATE: 1938

2 POSTER: LONDON
TRANSPORT
DATE: 1935

3 ADVERTISEMENT: SHELL OIL
DATE: 1937

3

1

2

Born in Nice, France. Trained at
the Ecole des Beaux-Arts, Lyon.
He first practised as a graphic
artist in Switzerland before
settling in Paris. From 1922
he was designing advertising
materials for a number of
French firms, including Voisin,
Monsavon and Vichy-Celestin.
Loupot's major contribution to a
totally new approach to poster
advertising came with the
commission in 1938 to redesign
the St Raphael-Quinquina
poster. He devised a strongly
graphic representation of the St
Raphael name. Once established
in the public eye, this was
broken up into formal patterns
and abstract designs which,
though no longer displaying the
full name, remained instantly
identifiable with it. This work
extended over almost 20 years,
but Loupot's output was varied
and extended into different
styles and contexts. In 1931,
he shared an exhibition of
poster art with Cassandre
and his work was included in
exhibitions of advertising art
worldwide. He contributed work
to, among others, La Gazette
du Bon Ton, Femina and Art et
Industrie.

1 ADVERTISEMENT: CAILLER
CHOCOLATE
DATE: 1921

2 ADVERTISEMENT: VALISÈRE
LINGERIE
DATE: 1937

3 ADVERTISEMENT:
VALENTINE PRINT
DATE: 1929

3

ERNEST HOWARD SHEPARD
(1879-1976)

Born in London. Educated at St Pauls School, where his early talent for drawing was encouraged. He took extra classes at Heatherley's Art School and in 1897 won a scholarship to the Royal Academy Schools, where he was the Landseer scholar in 1899. He began drawing for Punch *in 1907, and in 1945 became their chief cartoonist, which he remained until he was sacked by Malcolm Muggeridge in 1953. He produced some impressive political cartoons during World War 11, but his sensitive pen and ink style was more suited to childhood scenes and he is best remembered for his illustrations for A A Milne's* Winnie-the-Pooh *(1926) and Kenneth Grahame's* The Wind in the Willows *(1931).*

1-2 *BOOK:* THE WIND IN THE WILLOWS *by Kenneth Grahame*
DATE: 1931

3 *BOOK:* WHEN WE WERE VERY YOUNG *by A A Milne*
DATE: 1924

4-5 *BOOK:* WINNIE-THE-POOH *by A A Milne*
DATE: 1926

1

2

4

3

5

1   2

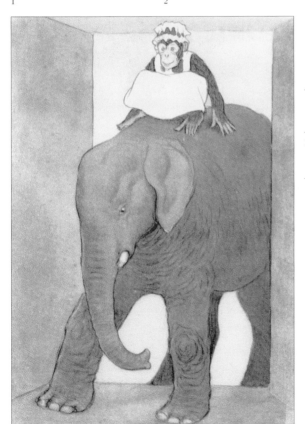

Born in Fair Oak, UK. Studied at New Cross Art School and the Royal College of Art, London. Married WE Webster, portrait painter and illustrator. Her distinctive style of children's book illustration shows a charmingly decorative approach to form and composition coupled with a sturdy sense of realistic detail. She illustrated several books, including Dickens' Captain Boldheart *(1927), and contributed to the periodical* Little Folks *and to* Playbox Annual, *but is particularly known for her series of* Ameliaranne *books, in which her illustrations were provided with texts by various writers, including Eleanor Farjeon and M Gilmour. Her 1920 poster illustration for Start-Rite shoes has become a classic graphic image.*

1, 2 *BOOK:* AMELIARANNE AT THE FARM *by M Gilmour*
DATE: 1937

3 *BOOK:* AMELIARANNE GIVES A CONCERT *by M Gilmour*
DATE: PUBLISHED 1944

3

ZERO
(1898-1976)

Born Hans Schleger in Kempen, Germany. Studied in Berlin and worked for five years in the USA, initially as a freelance designer and then as director of a New York advertising agency, where he adopted the name "Zero" when signing his work. In 1932 he moved to London and became a British citizen in 1938. He established his own studio and design consultancy and his work covered the full spectrum of graphic and commercial art. He was influenced by the Bauhaus, A M Cassandre and his close friend E McKnight Kauffer. As well as designing posters for clients such as Shell MacFisheries, London Transport and the Post Office, he pioneered the concept of corporate identity in the UK, illustrated book jackets, designed exhibitions and packaging and created the symbol for London bus stops and the trademark for Penguin books. He lectured at Chelsea School of Art and his work has been exhibited worldwide.

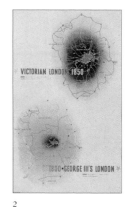

1

2

3

1 *POSTER:* LONDON PASSENGER TRANSPORT BOARD
DATE: 1936

2 *POSTER:* LONDON TRANSPORT
DATE: 1936

3 *POSTER:* LONDON UNDERGROUND
DATE: 1935

4 *POSTER:* SHELL FUEL
DATE: 1938

5 *POSTER:* LONDON TRANSPORT
DATE: 1939

6 *PUBLIC INFORMATION POSTER*
DATE: c. 1938

4

5

6

*Born in Basle, Switzerland.
Studied at the German
School of Art in Basle and the
Conservatory of Art in Zurich,
under Dr Oskar Bätschmann.
He taught for three years before
travelling to Paris in 1894,
where he began painting; and
subsequently to Munich, where
he mastered the technical
skills of lithography. In 1900
he returned to Basle and began
producing posters with a
graphic artist called Anstalten
Wassermann, Mangold was
extremely versatile and
employed a broad range of
styles to suit differing subjects.
In 1905 an exhibition of his
work was held in Zurich and
over the following 15 years he
established himself as one of the
most important poster artists of
his generation, producing some
of his finest work in the years
before World War I. In 1915 he
returned to the German School
of Art in Basle to study stained
glass design and lithography
and was president of the school
from 1918-29.*

1 *ADVERTISEMENT
DATE:* 1902

2 *ADVERTISEMENT
DATE:* 1916

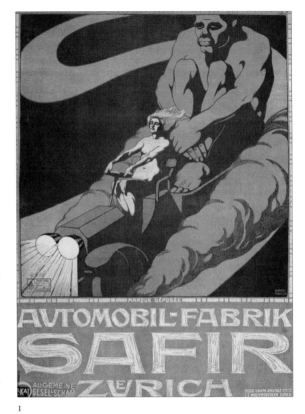

1

2

1   2

⊖ London Transport for all occasions

3

*Born in London. Studied at
Goldsmith's College School of
Art, The Royal College of Art
and the Central School of Arts
and Crafts in London. Her
books as author and illustrator
include* The Cross-Purposes
(1945), Ella's Birthday *(1946)
and* Beauty and the Burglar
(1958). *She contributed to*
Country Fair *and* The Strand
Magazine. *Her quirky,* faux-naif
*style was used to good effect
in London Transport posters
during the late 1930s, including
"London Transport for all
occasions", depicting a wedding
in which the bride and groom
are upstaged by several pale
bridesmaids and five angular
black cats. Animals were
favourite subjects and another
London Transport poster, "To
the fields", shows a complex
pattern of horses and frolicking
rabbits, typically combining an
aura of innocence with a sharp
visual wit.*

1 *POSTER:* LONDON
TRANSPORT
DATE: NOT KNOWN

2 *POSTER:* LONDON
TRANSPORT
DATE: 1938

3 *POSTER:* LONDON
TRANSPORT
DATE: 1938

WILLIAM HEATH ROBINSON
(1872-1944)

Born in London. After studying at the Royal Academy Schools he began illustrating books, including two children's books of his own, Uncle Lubin *(1902) and* Bill the Minder *(1912). During World War I he emerged as one of the greatest comic artists of his time with his whimsical pen and ink drawings of incredibly complicated contraptions usually designed to solve very simple problems. These drawings can be seen in* The Saintly Hum *(1917),* Humours of Golf *(1923),* Absurdities *(1934) and the* Professor Branestawm *books (1933), which finally made him the most famous of the three Robinson brothers, the others being Tom and Charles. Between the wars he contributed to such periodicals as* The Bystander, The Sketch, The Humorist, The Graphic *and* The Strand, *and exhibited a mural for the liner* Empress of Britain. *He worked mainly in black and white, and had a highly developed eye for detail and characterization.*

1 *BOOK:* THE INCREDIBLE ADVENTURES OF PROFESSOR BRANESTAWM
DATE: 1933

1

1

2

A group of Russian artists comprising Mikhail Kupriyanov (1903-1991), Porfiry Krylov (1902-1990) and Nikolai Sokolov (1903-2000). They studied at Vkhutemas in Moscow, where they were pupils of David Moor. During the 1920s they began to collaborate on student publications, first of all as "the Kukryniks", and after 1927, as "the Kukryniksy". From 1933 their cartoons began to appear regularly in Pravda and their satirical drawings were much in demand by leading newspapers and magazines. Their poster, "We shall mercilessly defeat and destroy the enemy", was one of the first to appear within a few days of Hitler's invasion and throughout World War II they made a significant contribution to Soviet political poster design. They were also prominent book illustrators.

1 CARICATURE: (published in Moscow)
DATE: c. 1940

2 CARICATURE: (published in Moscow)
DATE: c. 1940

3 CARICATURE: (published in Moscow)
DATE: c. 1940

3

JOHN HEARTFIELD
(1891-1968)

Born Helmut Herzfelde in Berlin. Studied at the School of Applied Arts in Munich and the Arts and Crafts School in Berlin. Later he Anglicized his name as a protest against German militarism. In 1911 he was one of the founders of the Berlin Dada group, and is renowned as the greatest exponent of photomontage – the technique of combining strikingly incongruous photographic images to surreal effect. An active member of the Communist Party *from 1918, he co-edited the satirical Journals* Jedermann Sein Eigener Fussball *and* Die Pleite *with Grosz and his brother, Wieland Herzfelde, and from 1923-27 was editor of the satirical magazine* Der Knüppel. *His anti-Nazi images, which appeared in most of the newspapers and magazines of the political left in Germany from the 1920s, lost him his German nationality in 1934. He was eventually forced to move to Czechoslovakia and then to Britain, where he worked for* Picture Post *and* Lilliput *magazines and Penguin Books. He returned to East Berlin in 1950. In 1956 he was nominated by Bertolt Brecht to the German Academy of Arts, where he became a professor.*

1 *ORIGINAL PHOTOMONTAGE:*
"BLOOD AND IRON"
DATE.-c. 1935

2 *ORIGINAL PHOTOMONTAGE*
DATE: 19 33

3 *ORIGINAL PHOTOMONTAGE*
DATE: 1934

4 *ORIGINAL PHOTOMONTAGE*
DATE.c. 1935

5 *MAGAZINE:* ARENA
DATE: 1927

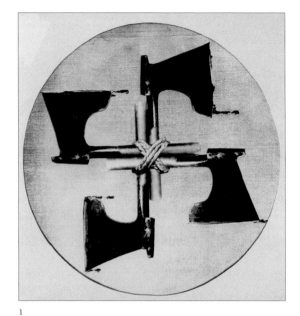

1

Deutſche
Eicheln
1933

2

3

4

5

Born in Montana, USA. He attended evening classes at the Mark Hopkins Institute, where he met Professor Joseph McKnight, who sponsored him to study art in Paris and whose name Kauffer adopted in tribute. From 1926-31 he was involved in theatre and exhibition design, interior design and book illustration. A great fan of T S Eliot's, he illustrated several of his books, including A Song for Simeon *(1925),* Ariel Poems *(1927) and* Marina *(1930). Such was Eliot's satisfaction that he wrote to Kauffer "Yours is the only kind of decoration I can endure." According to the art historian Anthony Blunt, Kauffer's posters and illustrations took the conventions of super-realism and cubism and broadened their appeal to an otherwise disinterested public. He spent two years in Paris before settling in London in 1914, where his posters for the Underground Railways and Shell Petroleum made him a national figure by the 1920s.*

1 *BOOK:* ELSIE AND THE CHILD *by Arnold Bennett*
DATE.1924

2 *POSTER:* LONDON TRANSPORT
DATE:1932

3 *TRAVEL POSTER*
DATE: c. 1924

4 *POSTER:* LONDON TRANSPORT
DATE.1954

5 *POSTER:* LONDON TRANSPORT
DATE: 1932

6 *ADVERTISEMENT:* SHELLFUEL
DATE: 1939

1

2

3

4

5

6

MAURITS CORNELIS ESCHER
(1898-1972)

*Born in Leeuwarden, Holland.
Studied graphics at the
Technical School of Architecture
and Ornamental Design in
Haarlem. Between 1922 and
1935 he experimented with
various graphic techniques,
producing about 70 woodcuts
and 40 lithographs during this
period. From 1938 he developed
highly decorative designs that
involved transformations of
form through mathematically
precise progressions. He
also produced a series of
geometric drawings, with
such titles as "The Regular
Division Of A Plane" and
"Cubic Space-division", which
were of particular interest to
mathematicians: a large number
of them were exhibited at the
International Mathematical
Congress in Amsterdam in 1964.
His hyper-realistic style had the
surreal effect of confusing the
real with the imaginary, as in
his complex and highly detailed
visual illusions which use
tricks of line and perspective to
create images of the impossible.
Since his death, his work has
frequently been used to illustrate
album covers, books and
magazine articles and his visual
ideas have been a source of
inspiration to photographers as
well as illustrators.*

1 *WOODCUT:* "DAY AND
NIGHT"
DATE: 1938

2 *WOODCUT:* "DEVELOPMENT
1"
DATE: 1937

1

2

1

2

3

Sir William Nicholson (1872-1949) and James Pryde (1886-1941). Although referred to as "The Beggarstaff Brothers", William Nicholson and James Pryde were in fact brothers-in-law. Nicholson was born in Newark-on-Trent, UK, and studied at the Académie Julien in Paris. Pryde, born in St Andrews, Scotland studied at the Royal Scottish Academy School in Paris under Bouguereau and then also at the Académie Julien. Their collaboration started when they entered a poster competition at the Westminister Aquarium. For economy's sake they worked in one colour and painted in silhouette for ease of reproduction. The ensuing success in the competition and the style that emerged from its constraints made them the most popular artists in Britain. As well as designing posters they both worked in theatre design and Nicholson was also a landscape, still-life and portrait painter who illustrated An Alphabet *(1898) and Siegfried Sassoon's* Memoirs of a Fox-Hunting Man *(1929).*

1 *THEATRE POSTER*
DATE: c. 1900

2 *PUBLICITY POSTER:*
HARPER'S MAGAZINE
DATE: c. 1900

3 *POSTCARD:* "CELEBRATED
POSTERS" SERIES
DATE: c. 1900

Born Dmitri Stakhievich Orlov in Russia. Studied law at Moscow university and dreamed of being an opera singer. However, after joining an insurgent group during the Moscow uprising of 1905, he helped to set up an underground print shop. The following year, an idle sketch he had made of a Tsarist minister was discovered by the editor of an evening newspaper and led to his first commission. He became a political cartoonist and produced a satirical review called Volynka that never passed the censors. After the October Revolution Moor concentrated on poster art and throughout the civil war years produced over 50 political posters. He always signed them, originally with the name Dor (an abbreviation of his real name), then Mor (to avoid confusion with a prominent journalist) and finally Moor (after a character in Schiller's play The Robbers). He was strongly influenced by French painting German graphic art and by the cartoonist Olaf Gulbransson.

1 *POSTER:* "TSARIST REGIMENTS & THE RED ARMY: WHAT THEY FOUGHT FOR BEFORE/ WHAT THEY FIGHT FOR NOW"
DATE: 1919

2 *POSTER:* "RED SOLDIER UNCLOAKS WRANGEL TO REVEAL CONSPIRACY OF WESTERN NATIONS AGAINST RUSSIA"
DATE: 1920

1

2

1

2

3

4

VIKTOR NIKOLAEVICH DENI
(1893-1946)

Born Viktor Denisov in Moscow. At the age of 17 he had his first drawings published in the satirical journal Budilink, *for which his older brother wrote poetry. In 1913 he moved to St Petersburg, where his work appeared regularly in the satirical journals* Solntse Rossii, Vesna *and* Satirikon, *and became art director of the humorous weekly* Bich. *When the magazine was closed down after the October Revolution, Deni began working for the artistic section of the Volga military district, making nearly 50 political posters between 1918 and 1921 and becoming one of the leading figures in Soviet poster art (the other was David Moor), particularly admired for his satirical eye. From 1921 he concentrated on drawing newspaper cartoons, contributing regularly to* Pravda, *the Party newspaper, until World War II, when he went back to making posters.*

1 *POSTER:* DEMKEN'S BAND"
DATE: 1919

2 *POSTER:* "AT THE GRAVE OF COUNTER-REVOLUTION"
DATE: 1920

3 *POSTER:* "CAPITAL"
DATE: 1919

4 *POSTER:* "CONSTITUENT ASSEMBLY MEETING"
DATE: 1921

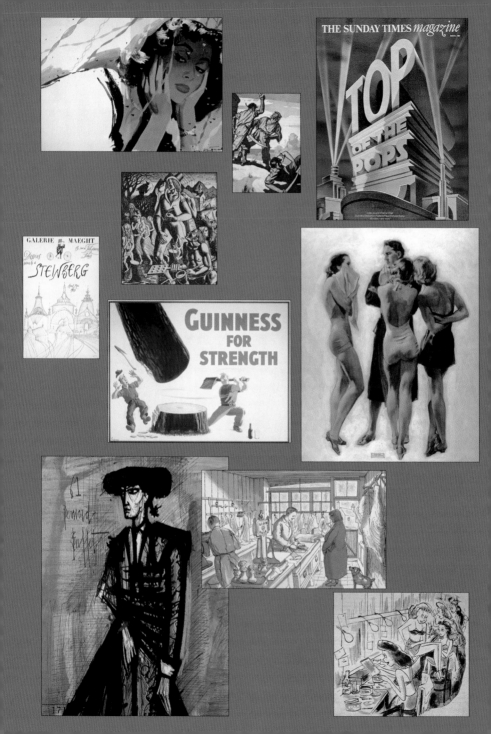

CHAPTER THREE

AS FAR AS ILLUSTRATION WAS CONCERNED, the onset of World War II presented a set of opportunities as well as a set of limitations. The need for propaganda, morale boosting and public information material generated a great deal of work. Surprisingly, advertising also thrived during this period. Many manufacturers were concerned that the public would forget them while their production was limited and so ran long-term branding campaigns that stressed their own efforts in the war and assured customers that both quality and supply would be restored as soon as the war had ended.

But while the conflict kept artists busy, the shortages of working materials had a direct effect on their style and methods of working. Paper shortages necessitated that magazines be printed on thinner stock, and art directors advised their illustrators to avoid heavy contrast in their images as the darker areas would print through and appear on the other side of the page. It also became common to print on the reverse side of unused posters, and this encouraged artists to use darker colours to ensure that the old image could not be seen.

With the end of the war, the mid-1940s became boom years for the illustrator in America. During this period of social reconstruction, publishers placed a great emphasis on "lifestyle", and developed a close relationship with the American housewife through magazines such as *Cosmopolitan* and *Ladies' Home Journal,* which featured the work of artists such as John La Gatta and Jon Whitcomb. At the same time, Norman Rockwell was becoming famous for his portraits of American life, which were featured regularly on the covers of the *Saturday Evening Post.* Advertising budgets rocketed, and the hyper-realistic effect of the airbrush challenged photography in the multitude of campaigns mounted by the fast-growing motor car industry. Even the illustrated novel enjoyed a revival with the arrival of the book club.

The 1950s, however, saw a reaction against slick, photograph-oriented realism. The invention of television had a disastrous effect on the publishing business, and several national periodicals folded. There was also a sharp decline in the sale of illustrated books, due to the prevalent belief that a novelist's imagination should be interpreted by the reader and not by an illustrator. In aesthetic terms these problems created a very positive energy and response as publishers adopted a more progressive attitude and took artistic risks in the hope of regaining their fickle public. The result was a diversity of styles, which was encouraged also by the presence of European artists, such as George Grosz, who had emigrated to America at the end of World War II.

Throughout this time in Britain, the illustrator's life had been running on a parallel course to that on the other side of the Atlantic. During the war years, government spending had encouraged the work of many artists, including Abram Games, Tom

Eckersley, McKnight Kauffer and Fougasse and, with the return of peace, advertising clients clamoured for their services. In their hands, and with the sponsorship of major companies such as Shell, the poster regained its status as an art form.

There was also something of a revival of book illustration within the Neo-Romantic style. This lasted for about 12 years and began with the publication in 1943 of Mervyn Peake's illustrations for Coleridge's *Rime of the Ancient Mariner*. However, the introduction of British television in the 1950s damaged the publishing industry in much the way it had done in America, although it led to an increased circulation of the *Radio Times* magazine, which was then, and remains, a particularly good medium for the introduction of new illustrator's work.

The complacency, born of prosperity that suffused this period could never have prepared either artists or the public for the style revolution that was to take place in the 1960s.

Pop Art actually began its life in 1956, not in America but in Britain, with Richard Hamilton's photomontages parodying the domestic and materialistic lifestyle of the time. His work, and that of others in the Independent Group, was further developed in the early '60s by artists such as David Hockney, Patrick Caulfield and Allen Jones in the UK and Andy Warhol in America. Simultaneously, Bridget Riley, Peter Sedgley and Piero Dorazio were exploring the optical effects of line and colour first seen in the paintings of the Spanish artist Victor Vasarely. The philosophies and aesthetics of these artists then meshed with the emergence of a counter-culture that expressed its anarchic sensibilities through every conceivable medium: paintings, sculpture, music, illustrations, fashion, underground magazines, poster art, festivals and "happenings".

What followed was an explosion of aesthetic extravagance never seen before. Naturalistic colours were replaced with day-glow psychedelia in the works of Victor Moscoso and Martin Sharp. Michael English's rock n roll posters, which revealed the influence of Art Nouveau, featured convoluted and virtually unreadable hand-rendered lettering. Eclecticism was the guiding principle of the day: Eastern imagery, mysticism and hallucinatory experience were major creative influences in all branches of the arts.

This revolution was not confined to the so-called "underground". It affected every level of society and, through the work of artists such as Milton Glaser and the influential Push Pin Studios, it reached every level of mainstream media. If ever there was a lingering question about the status of the illustrator as artist, it was answered in the 1960s.

CHAPTER THREE

Studied at the Slade School of Fine Art. Marshall developed a very fluid black-and-white style in charcoal and pen and ink which earned him many commissions for fashion illustrations in the 1950s. His drawings were full of movement and captured the energy and elegance of the catwalk models and of the era, and his work dominated the pages of Vogue, Harper's Bazaar *and* Woman's Journal. *In 1950 he wrote and illustrated* Sketching the Ballet, *and later produced similar volumes entitled* Fashion Drawing *and* Drawing the Female Figure. *In his manual* Magazine Illustration *(1959) he encouraged the use of photographs as reference material and recommended the special "incident" studios that were then producing images for illustrators. He was also an accomplished water colourist and landscape artist and exhibited several times at London's Walker Galleries.*

1 *MAGAZINE:* WOMAN'S MAGAZINE
DATE: c. 1950

2 *MAGAZINE:* WOMAN'S MAGAZINE
DATE: 1950

The New York skyline from the decks of *Queen Elizabeth* as she leaves Pier 90—a sketch by Francis Marshall

1

2

1

Born in Naples, Italy. Emigrated
to America and studied at the
Chase School New York School
of Applied and Fine Arts,
Parsons and the Art Students
League. He began his career in
advertising illustration before
establishing his own studio in
Woodstock, where he specialized
in illustrations of beautiful
women. Advised by his wife and
model Florence, his drawings
of romantic interludes among
the upper classes regularly
illustrated the stories in
magazines such as Redbook,
Ladies' Home Journal and
Cosmopolitan and he received
many commissions in the early
years of World War II. In 1941
he moved to California, where
he took up portraiture and
landscape painting.

1 MAGAZINE: REDBOOK
DATE: c. 1940

2 MAGAZINE: COSMOPOLITAN
DATE: 1949

3 MAGAZINE: REDBOOK
DATE: c. 1940

2

3

1

2

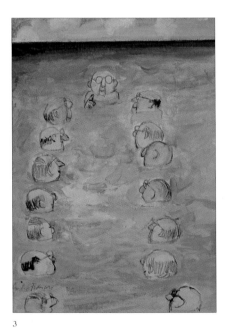

3

4

ANDRE FRANCOIS
(1915- 2005)

5

6

7

*Born in Timisoara, Hungary.
Studied in Budapest, then
under Cassandre in Paris.
From 1944 he established
himself as a humorous artist
and his distinctive, satirical
images appeared in magazines
such as* Punch, Vogue *and* New
Yorker. *His advertising posters
for Citroën and Kodak are
among the most innovative and
influential of the 20th century.
Francois was also a sculptor
and poster artist and designed
stage sets and costumes for
the theatre and ballet. His own
illustrated books included*
The Tattooed Sailor *and Other
Cartoons from France (1953),*
The Half-naked Knight *(1958),*
The Biting Eye *(1960) and*
Les Rhumes *(1966). He also
illustrated* Ubu Roi *by Alfred
Jarry (1957).*

1 *ADVERTISEMENT:* CITROËN
CARS
DATE: 1960

2 *ADVERTISEMENT:* CITROEN
CARS
DATE: 1960

3 *MAGAZINE:* THE NEW
YORKER
DATE: 1965

4 "FIRST AID FORTHE
DROWNED" *(unpublished)*
DATE: 1947

5 *MAGAZINE:* PUNCH
DATE: 1955

6 *MAGAZINE:* PUNCH
DATE: 1960

7 "BIG RED BICYCLE"
(unpublished)
DATE: 1955

Born in Lancashire, UK. Trained at Salford School of Art under Martin Tyas. He moved to London in 1934 and set up in partnership with Eric Lombers. In 1935 he won the Heywood Medal of Merit for poster design and from 1937-39 he taught poster art at Westminster School of Art. Like his contemporary, Abram Games, Eckersley produced posters with simple graphic imagery, integrated typography, clean lines and strong colours. During World War II he produced cartographical drawings for the Royal Air Force, returning to freelance design in 1945. His style attracted many advertising clients, including Gillette, Guinness, British Aluminium, Eno's and various cigarette brands. In 1948 he was awarded the OBE for his services to British poster design and in 1958 became Head of Graphic Design at the London College of Printing.

1 *PUBLIC INFORMATION POSTER:* ROYAL SOCIETY FOR THE PREVENTION OF ROAD ACCIDENTS, LONDON
DATE: 1944

2 *WWII POSTER:* POST OFFICE SAVINGS BANK
DATE: 1943

1

2

1

2

3

4

Born in Haiphong, Vietnam. His family moved to England when he was five. Attended life classes at Westminster School of Art, under Bernard Meninsky, while employed as a clerk in the City. At the age of 27 he gave up his job to become an artist, and around 1930 began illustrating regularly for the Radio Times. His books Little Tim and the Brave Sea Captain (1936) and Lucy Brown and Mr Grimes (1937), which he wrote and illustrated to entertain his own children, were a great success in England and America and Tim All Alone (1956), was the first book to win the British Library Association's Kate Greenaway Medal. He is best known as a children's illustrator, but his fluid and expressive style, either drawn with cross-hatching or painted in simple watercolours, was equally suited to serious subjects. He cited Bernard Meninsky, Doré, Daumier and Caldecott as his main influences. He was an Official War Artist during World War II and the drawings he made remain a powerful record of the atrocities of war.

1 ADVERTISEMENT: PUNCH
MAGAZINE
DATE: 1954

2 ADVERTISEMENT: GUINNESS
BEER
DATE: 1955

3 ADVERTISEMENT: GUINNESS
BEER
DATE: 1955

4 BOOK: TIM ALL ALONE by
Edward Ardizzone
DATE: 1956

Born in Kuling, China, the son
of medical missionaries. The
family returned to England
in 1923 and he was educated
at Eltham College, Kent, and
the Royal Academy Schools in
London. His first illustrated
book, Captain Slaughterboard, a
humorous fantasy for children,
was published in 1939.
Invalided out of the forces in
1943, he visited Germany in
1946 to record the devastation
for Leader magazine. He was
also sent to make drawings at
Belsen – an experience which
profoundly affected his later
work. Peake illustrated many
books, including Alice Through
the Looking Glass (1954),
Grimm's Fairy Tales and
Treasure Island. He also wrote
and illustrated his own novels
and poems, including Rhymes
Without Reason (1944), Captain
Slaughterboard Drops Anchor
(1945), Shapes and Sounds
(1941) and The Glassblowers
(1950). His most famous work,
Gormenghast (part two of a
gothic fantasy trilogy written
between 1946 and 1959) won
the W J Heinemann Foundation
Prize (Royal Society of
Literature) in 1950. In many of
Peake's works a lively humour
is merged with an instinct for
the macabre and the grotesque,
as seen in the facial caricatures
that were a recurring element in
his work.

1,4-6 BOOK: RIDE-A-COCK
HORSE & OTHER NURSERY
RHYMES
DATE: 1945

2, 7 BOOK: FIGURES OF
SPEECH by Mervyn Peake
DATE: 1952

3 BOOK: TITUS ALONE by
Mervyn Peake
DATE: 1959

1

Coming up to scratch

2

3

4

5

6

7

PHILIP GOUGH
(b. 1908)

Born in Warrington, Cheshire, UK. Studied at art schools in Liverpool London and Penzance and trained as a stage designer in Liverpool. In 1928 he designed the sets for A Midsummer Night's Dream *at Liverpool Repertory Theatre and in 1929 designed the sets for the original production of* Toad of Toad Hall. *Moving to London, he worked in a commercial studio for two years and then began designing for the London theatres, working on over 25 productions until after World War II, when he turned to book and magazine illustration.*

1 *BOOK:* THE NEW BOOK OF DAYS
DATE: 1941

2, 3 *BOOK:* HANS AND ERSEN'S FAIRY TALES
DATE: 1946

1

2

3

1

2

Born in Long Island, USA,
but settled in England
during childhood. Studied at
Goldsmith's College School
of Art, London, and won a
travelling scholarship which he
applied to studying marine art
in the Netherlands. From 1925
he received commissions from
publishers, many with marine
themes, including Moby Dick
(1926) and The Adventures
of a Trafalgar Lad (1926). His
landscape drawings for Mary
Webb's Precious Bane (1929)
were later marketed as greetings
cards. Other significant titles
were The Midnight Folk (1931),
a personal commission from
poet laureate John Masefield,
The Bible for Today (1938)
and with his wife Edith Wider,
the Shell Guide to Flowers of
the Countryside. His prolific
output of greetings card designs
for the Medici Society and
Ward Gallery established his
widespread popularity, but
after World War II he published
his designs through his own
Heron Press. From the 1960s
he became increasingly more
dedicated to painting for non-
commercial reasons, though his
work continued to be widely
reproduced.

1 *MAGAZINE:* PUNCH
DATE: 1952

2-3 *BOOK:* TREASURE ISLAND
by Robert Louis Stevenson
DATE: 1946

3

Born in Basel, Switzerland. Studied at art schools in Munich and Basel. He was a major figure in the development of Swiss poster art, which had already achieved high standards by the 1920s. His work produced a refinement of design concepts, ranging from stylised, two-dimensional almost purely symbolic images to more detailed and realistic representations, married to clean, unfussy typographic presentation. Examples can be seen in museums in Basel and Zurich, and Stoecklin's work has gone into private collections worldwide. Another important interest was postage stamp design and he produced a number of detailed designs for this purpose, mainly featuring plants and animals. He also illustrated books, including Hermann Hesse's Knulp *(1945).*

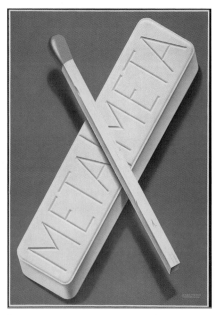

1

1 *ADVERTISEMENT:* BINACA
TOOTHPASTE
DATE: 1941

2 *ADVERTISEMENT:* META
MATCH STRIKERS
DATE: 1941

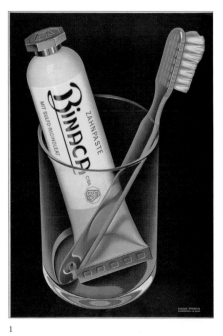

2

Born in Cambridge, UK. Studied painting at art schools in England and Paris. After settling in London, from 1901 he worked on The Illustrated London News, *an association lasting almost 15 years. He also contributed to* The Graphic, The Harmsworth Magazine *and* The Illustrated Mail. *He was an accomplished marine painter and his book illustrations covered naval subjects, landscapes and angling themes.* Landscapes and Seascapes *(1929) and* Ships in Pictures *(1944) were among his own published titles. During both World Wars he designed the camouflage used by British Navy ships. It was at Wilkinson's suggestion that in the 1920s London Midland & Scottish Railways commissioned posters from a number of notable artists of the day, including Fred Taylor and Tom Purvis. His own "Galloway" (1924) is a graphic portrait of the rich colour and expanse of the Scottish Highlands. He was also commissioned for poster work by the shipping company Cunard.*

1 *TRAVEL POSTER:* LONDON MIDLAND & SCOTTISH RAILWAY COMPANY
DATE: 1940

2 *PUBLIC INFORMATION POSTER*
DATE: 1940

3 *TRAVEL POSTER:* LONDON MIDLAND & SCOTTISH RAILWAY COMPANY
DATE: NOT KNOWN

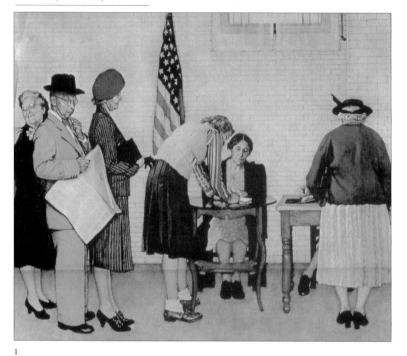

1

2

3

4

5

*Born in New York. Studied at
Chase Art School, the National
Academy of Design and the
Art Students League in New
York, under Thomas Fogarty
and George Bridgman. At
the age of 17 he was already
illustrating for McBride and
Nast publications and later
became editor of a boy scout's
magazine. His covers for*
The Saturday Evening Post,
*spanning more than 40 years
from 1916, made him one of
America's best-known and most
loved illustrators. His superbly
crafted portrayals of American
life were done with a warmth
and humour that touched the
hearts of millions and reflected
the spirit of the country at the
time. During World War II the
essence of Franklin D Roosevelt's
war aims was captured in
Rockwell's powerful* Four
Freedoms *posters, one of which
is on permanent display at the
Metropolitan Museum of Art in
New York.*

1 *MAGAZINE:* THE SATURDAY
EVENING POST
DATE: 1940

2 *MAGAZINE:* THE SATURDAY
EVENING POST
DATE: c. 1940

3 *POSTER*
DATE: c. 1945

4 *MAGAZINE:* THE SATURDAY
EVENING POST
DATE: 1940

5 *MAGAZINE:* THE SATURDAY
EVENING POST
DATE. 1949

BEN SHAHN
(1898- 1969)

*Born in Kovno, Russia. His
family emigrated to America
in 1904 and he studied biology
at New York University and
attended the National Academy
of Design. In the 1920s he
travelled in Europe and North
Africa and during World War II
he designed posters for various
government departments.
His work, which used heavy
outlines to expressive effect
and which brought to mind
the illustrations of Francois
and Buffet, has won numerous
awards. He illustrated several
children's books, including* A
Partridge in a Pear Tree *(1949),
which featured illustrations in a
style that was most unusual for
the world of the nursery rhyme.
His adult publications include*
The Sorrows of Priapus *(1957)
by E Dahlberg and* Thirteen
Poems *(1956) by Wilfred Owen.
His work also appeared in
advertising campaigns and in
publications such as* Fortune
Magazine, Harper's Bazaar *and*
Town and Country. *He was a
painter as well as an illustrator
and had one-man shows in
Boston, New York and Chicago.*

1

1 *WWII POSTER*
DATE: 1943

2 *WWII POSTER*
DATE: 1943

2

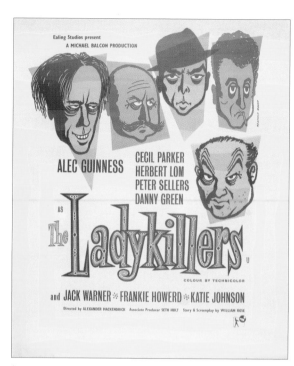

1

Born in London. Studied at Leyton School of Art. Mount worked at Greenly's studio in London, then as a visualiser at the Lintas advertising agency, before being employed at Odhams Press Ltd as a general artist and designer. During World War II he worked for the Ministry of Information, where he produced some of Britain's finest war posters, including the salvage, security and diptheria immunisation campaigns and the first national anti-VD campaign in 1943-44. He also designed the "Liberation of France" poster for the D-Day landings. After the war he worked as a freelance designer in house-styling, packaging, publicity and exhibitions, while continuing part-time at what became the Central Office of Information. With Eileen Evans, he produced an enormous body of work, including award-winning posters for the anti-smoking and road safety campaigns and the now classic "Keep Britain Tidy" campaign. In 1957 he was awarded the OBE for services to government publicity.

1 FILM POSTER: LADYKILLERS
DATE: 1955

2 GOVERNMENT INFORMATION
POSTER
DATE: 1962

3 GOVERNMENT INFORMATION
POSTER
DATE: 1943

2

3

FOUGASSE
(1887-1965)

Born Cyril Kenneth Bird, in London, and educated at Cheltenham College and King's College, London. From 1916 his work was published in Punch *and in 1937 he became its Art Editor, then Editor (1949-52). He illustrated a number of books, including* The Luck of the Draw *(1936),* Drawing the Line Somewhere *(1937) and* The Good Tempered Pencil *(1956). During World War II he designed posters for various government ministries, including the famous "Careless Talk Costs Lives" series for the Ministry of Information. Fougasse was a master of the expressive line. Over the years he developed a highly individual graphic shorthand in his drawings of humorous figures, the hands and feet often represented by a single line.*

1 *WWII POSTER*
DATE: 1940

2 *WWII POSTER*
DATE: 194 0

3 *POSTER:* LONDON
UNDERGROUND
DATE: c. 1940

4 POSTER: NATIONAL SOCIETY
FOR THE PREVENTION OF
CRUELTY TO CHILDREN
DATE: c. 1940

"*Of course there's no harm in* your *knowing!*"

CARELESS TALK COSTS LIVES

1

Pack up your problems in
SSAFA

2

PLEASE STAND ON THE RIGHT
OF THE ESCALATOR

3

In 60 years,
NSPCC
has come to the rescue of
5¼ MILLION CHILDREN
PLEASE HELP US, IF YOU CAN

4

1

2

3

RONALD SEARLE
(b. 1920)

*Born in Cambridge, UK. Studied
at Cambridge School of Art and
first started drawing for the*
Cambridge Daily News *in 1935.
In 1939 he fought in Malaya
and was imprisoned by the
Japanese from 1942 onwards,
an experience which he cites as
a major formative experience.
His first published book after the
war,* Forty Drawings of Ronald
Searle *(1946), was a sobering
record of this bleak interlude
in his life. However, he is more
famous for having created
the St Trinian's schoolgirls
in his books* Hurrah for St
Trinian's *(1948),* The Female
Approach *(1948),* Back to the
Slaughterhouse, *(1952) and* The
Terror of St Trinian's *(1952). In
1956 he joined the staff of* Punch
*magazine, a perfect platform
for his witty observations on
social behaviour. His work also
had a serious side and he was
a member of the Association of
International Artists, a political
group. In 1969 he produced*
The Secret Sketchbook: The
Backstreets of Hamburg, *which
contained no text but a series
of expressive sketches of
prostitutes which owe something
to the influence of George Grosz.
His work has appeared in many
of the major British publications
and was frequently published
in America's* Saturday Evening
Post.

1 *ADVERTISEMENT*
DATE: 1960

2 "THE COMING OF THE
GREAT CAT GOD"
DATE: 1968

3 "ST TRINIAN'S"
DATE: c. 1948-1952

NOEL FONTANET
(1898-1982)

Born in Germany. Studied at the Geneva Art School and later drew for local newspapers and produced caricatures for the Nebelspalter. *He was an excellent draughts man and developed a strong graphic style which earned him the position of art director in a design company, and fame as a poster artist.*

1 *POSTER:* "GENEVA INTERNATIONAL AUTOMOBILE SHOW"
DATE: 1930

2 *ADVERTISEMENT:* VELOSOLEX
DATE: 1950

3 *POSTER:* "GIVE BOOKS"
DATE: 1943

1

2

3

KEITH VAUGHAN
(1912-1977)

1

2

Born in Sussex, UK. He received no formal art training but during the 1930s he developed an interest in modern art, particularly the work of Cezanne, Picasso and the French Impressionists. During World War II he worked as a clerk and German interpreter in London and produced a huge volume of powerful gouaches and ink drawings which were displayed as part of a war exhibition at the National Gallery. His first one-man show was in 1944 and it was at this time that he met Graham Sutherland and John Minton. During the 1950s his work, although essentially figurative, became more abstract and revealed the influence of De Stael and the Abstract Expressionists. He had several major exhibitions and taught periodically at the Camberwell, Central and Slade Schools of Art. In 1964 he was made an Honorary Fellow of the Royal College of Art and in 1965 was awarded the CBK. His Journals and Drawings were published the following year and in 1989 there was a major retrospective of his work at the Austin/Desmond Gallery in London.

1 "LANDSCAPE" (unpublished)
DATE: 1949

2 "THE WOODMAN"
(unpublished)
DATE: 1949

CHARLES KEEPING
(1924-1988)

Born in London. The son of a professional boxer, he grew up around the street markets of south London. After World War II he studied drawing, etching, engraving and lithography at the Regent Street Polytechnic where he returned in 1956 as a lecturer. Keeping works mostly in pen and ink he illustrated over 50 books, including Charlie, Charlotte and the Golden Canary, which won the Kate Greenaway Medal in 1967, and The Wildman, which won the Francis Williams Prize in 1976. Joseph's Yard (1969), The God Beneath the Sea (1970) and The Railway Passage (1974) were all commended for the Kate Greenaway Medal. He has taught at Camberwell School of Art since 1979 and his work is represented at the Victoria & Albert Museum in London.

1 "COSTER CART"
(unpublished)
DATE: 1956

2 "DERELICT CITY CARTS"
(unpublished)
DATE: 1954

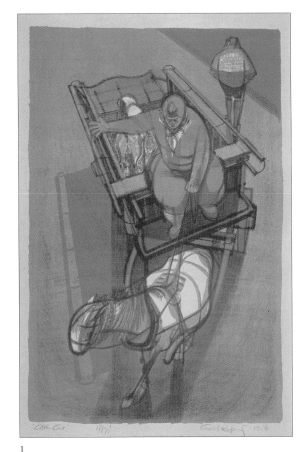

1

2

1

2

Born in Birkenhead, UK. He drew from childhood but was not encouraged to consider a career in art and started work in 1939 as a junior office clerk. After World War II a special government grant awarded to ex-servicemen enabled him to study at Liverpool College of Art and after graduating in 1950 he taught at Wolverhampton College of Art. In 1952 he sent his first cartoon to Punch magazine and in 1956 he left teaching to take up illustration full-time. Over the next 25 years he produced over 60 covers and 1500 illustrations for Punch, reflecting the English way of life. He also drew a pony cartoon strip, "Penelope and Kipper", for the Sunday Express. Although he is most famous for his humorous cartoons of endearingly scruffy, barrel-chested ponies ridden by tubby little girls, he also drew cartoons on a wide range of serious moral and political issues, but always with his characteristically gentle eye. His books are sold all over the world and his autobiography, Wrestling with a Pencil, was published in 1986.

1 "ACQUIRING A PONY IS NOT AS EASY AS IT SOUNDS"
DATE: 1962

2 "I NEVER TIRE OF LOOKING AT THE SEA"
DATE: 1952

FRANK FRAZETTA
(b. 1928)

Born in Brooklyn, New York. At
the age of only eight, he enrolled
at the Brooklyn Academy of
Fine Arts. He started his career
working in comics, was an
assistant to Al Capp on Li'l
Abner and developed his own
strip called Johnny Comet as
well as contributing to Mad and
Playboy. During the 60s and 70s
his cover illustrations for the
Conan series of heroic fantasy
stories by R E Howard brought
him to the forefront of science-
fiction art. After illustrating the
covers for a series of Tarzan
paperbacks his style changed
direction as he became more
involved in sword and sorcery
illustrations. From this genre
Frazetta has emerged as an
artist with a cult following.
He now has the freedom to
choose his own subjects and
the originals of his calendars,
posters and paperback covers
are valuable collectors' pieces.
His style, characterized by
exotic settings, sex, violence
and exaggerated physiques, is
definitive of fantasy art and has
been enormously influential The
Fantastic Art of Frank Frazetta
was published in 1975.

1

---

1 POSTER: "FRANKENSTEIN
AND DRACULA" (non-
commissioned)
DATE: 1969

---

2 POSTER: "REASSEMBLED
MAN" (non-commissioned)
DATE: 1965

---

3 POSTER: "THE RETURN OF
JOUGAR" (non-commissioned)
DATE: 1967

2

3

Born in Paris. At 15 he took evening classes in art and spent a year at the Ecole des Beaux-Arts in Paris. In 1947 he held his first exhibition, in a book shop in the Rue des Ecoles, and in 1948 shared the Grand Prix de la Critique. Seven years later his distinctive style won him recognition by the Connaissance des Arts as the leading post-war artist. His illustrated books included Cocteau's La Voix Humaine (1957), Cyrano de Bergerac's Les Voyages Fantastiques (1958) and Les Chants des Maldoror (1952). He has also designed stage sets for two ballets: La Chambre for Roland Petit and Le Rendezvous Manque, based on a story by Francoise Sagan. His work is held in permanent collection by the Tate Gallery, London, and the Museum of Modern Art, New York.

1 *CATALOGUE:* NICOLAS WINE
DATE: 1961

2 *POSTER:* "YOUNG PAINTER IN FRANCE"
DATE: 1955

3 *PAINTING:* "PIETA"
DATE: 1941

1

2

3

Born in London, daughter of the illustrator John Hassall. She studied at the Royal Academy Schools and subsequently attended the London County Council School of Photo-engraving and Lithography. Her first commission after graduating was for a wood-engraved title page for her brother Christopher's book of poems Devil's Dyke *(1936). Other books included* A Child's Garden of Verses *by Robert Louis Stevenson (1947) and Jane Austen's* Mansfield Park *(1959),* Northanger Abbey *(1960),* Persuasion *(1961) and* Emma *(1962). She also illustrated for a number of magazines, including* Argosy, London Mystery Magazine, Picture Post *and* The Periodical, *and designed the invitation for the coronation of Queen Elizabeth II in 1952. Her wood-engraved illustrations were worked in a meticulous style influenced by Thomas Bewick.*

---

1 *BOOK:* CRANFORD *by Mrs Gaskell*
DATE: 1940

---

2 *BOOK:* SEALSKIN TROUSERS
by Eric Linklater
DATE: 1947

---

3 *BOOK:* URANIA *by Ruth Pitter*
DATE: 1950

---

4 *BOOK:* COLLECTED POEMS
OF ANDREW YOUNG
DATE: 1950

1

3

2

4

1

3

Born in London. Mainly self-taught as an artist, his first job was in a commercial studio from 1932-36, and it was during this period that he developed an interest in poster design. His work, featuring striking colour, bold graphic ideas and beautifully integrated typography, communicated clearly and effectively, and in 1940 he became the official War Office poster designer. At the end of the war he produced posters and stamps for British, Irish, Israeli and Portuguese government departments, and designed murals and advertising poster campaigns for clients such as Guinness, BOAC, Shell and Capstan cigarettes. In 1951 he designed the official emblem for the Festival of Britain and in 1953 the symbol of BBC Television. From 1946-53 he taught at the Royal College of Art in London. He was awarded the OBE in 1958 for his services to graphic design.

1 *POSTER:* FINSBURY HEALTH CENTRE
DATE: 1943

2 *POSTER:* BRITISH EUROPEAN AIRWAYS
DATE: 1960

3 *POSTER:* LONDON TRANSPORT
DATE: 1953

Born in Beckenham, UK. Studied at Dulwich College and Goldsmith's College of Art, under Ed Sullivan. After graduation he designed scenery and costumes for the Everyman Theatre in Hampstead, London, then worked briefly in advertising before becoming a freelance illustrator. In 1934 he designed and executed a huge mural at the Museum of the Chartered Insurance Institute of London. From 1936-37 he lived in New York where he began writing and illustrating children's books. He specialized in historical reconstructions, and the publication of Shakespeare's Theatre won him the Kate Greenaway Medal for best British book illustration in 1964. In 1966 he was runner-up for the Carnegie Medal for Namesake. His love of the stage was quite evident in his work and in 1951 he was involved in the design of the Mermaid Theatre in London.

1 *MAGAZINE:* RADIO TIMES
DATE: 1950

2 *MAGAZINE:* RADIO TIMES
DATE: 1950

3 *MAGAZINE:* RADIO TIMES
DATE: 1950

Christmas Number with Programmes from Christmas Eve to December 30
WITH FULL DETAILS OF
'Christmas Journey' the world-wide programme preceding the broadcast by
H.M. THE KING

1

2   3

Born Victor Weisz in Berlin, of Hungarian parentage. He left school at the age of 14 to help support his family and began selling caricatures of public figures to the local newspapers. With the rise of Nazism he turned to political cartoons in 1929 and in 1935 he left Germany to settle in London, where he became a British citizen. He worked for the News Chronicle *as a staff artist and, in the years after World War II, his drawings illustrated stories and articles in publications such as* Cosmopolitan, Woman's Own, The Leader *and* The Daily Mirror *and in 1958 he joined the staff of the* Evening Standard.

1 *MAGAZINE:* THE LEADER
DATE: 1950

2 *MAGAZINE:* THE LEADER
DATE: 1950

1

2

LEONARD BASKIN
(1922-2000)

Born in New Brunswick, USA. Studied at Yale University of Fine Arts and the New School for Social Research, and also in Paris and Florence. Sculptor and graphic artist, he has made an important contribution to book illustration as publisher and printer for his own Gehenna Press. The first title of this imprint, On a Pyre of Withered Roses *(1942), was produced while Baskin was still a student at Yale. The range of subsequent work included strongly graphic linoleum and wood engravings in* A Little Book of Natural History *(1951), and highly detailed etchings in* Horned Beetles and Other Insects *(1958).*

1 "TOBIAS AND THE ANGEL"
(unpublished)
DATE: 1958

2 "MAN WITH SPRING PLANTS"
(unpublished)
DATE: 1953

1

2

1

Born in Ohio, USA. Trained at the Dayton Art Institute and the Chicago Art Institute, where he took evening classes while serving an apprenticeship in a local art studio. He worked briefly for the Herald Examiner *before moving to New York. In common with his contemporary, Jon Whitcomb, his primary interest was in depicting glamorous and beautiful women, but his softer use of colour was more definitively romantic and his compositions explored the subtler nuances of the relationships between men and women.*

1 *MAGAZINE:* LADIES' HOME JOURNAL
DATE: 1947

2 *ILLUSTRATION: (unpublished)*
DATE: NOT KNOWN

3 *MAGAZINE:* THE SATURDAY EVENING POST
DATE: NOT KNOWN

2

3

THORNTON UTZ
(1914- 1999)

Born in Memphis, USA. He was a student of Burton Callicott, whom he cites as his greatest influence, before attending the American Academy of Art in Chicago. He then became a freelance illustrator at the studio partnership of Sundblom, Stevens and Stultz. Although one of the "Sundblom Circle", he developed his own highly individual approach to the problems of illustration. His method was to work out his compositions with quick, rough sketches and then pose and photograph models in the positions that he has drawn. Later, when preparing the final illustration, he used the photographs to provide details of lighting and minutiae that would otherwise remain unseen. The technique was extremely successful and he was commissioned frequently by The Saturday Evening Post, Cosmopolitan, Redbook and Good Housekeeping. During the early 50s he travelled to India, Japan, Hong Kong and Hawaii recording the activities of the US Air Force. He now concentrates on commissioned portrait painting.

1 MAGAZINE: SPORTS AFIELD
DATE: 1959

2 MAGAZINE: THE SATURDAY
EVENING POST
DATE: 1962

3 MAGAZINE: THE SATURDAY
EVENING POST
DATE: 1958

1

2

3

1

2

Born in Oklahoma, USA. Studied art at Ohio Wesleyan University, then worked as a poster artist and produced drawings for local advertising agencies. In 1934 he moved to New York and concentrated on freelance illustration. He specialized in depicting romantic interludes and portraits of beautiful, glamorous women and achieved popularity through publication in such magazines as Collier's and Good Housekeeping. He spent some time as a combat artist during World War II, returning to gentler themes after his discharge in 1945. His style was perfectly suited to the editorial content of Redbook Magazine and Cosmopolitan, for whom he wrote and illustrated a monthly column on movie stars. He also wrote two children's books, Coco and Pom Pom's Christmas, and a book on beautiful women, All about Girls.

1 "BROWN-HAIRED GAL"
(unpublished)
DATE: c. 1940

2 MAGAZINE: WOMAN'S HOME
COMPANION
DATE: 1941

EDWARD BAWDEN
(1903-1989)

Born in Braintree, UK. Studied at Cambridge School of Art and the Royal College of Art, under Paul Nash. He was an Official War Artist during World War II and travelled to France and the Middle East. His strong graphic style, economy of line and sardonic wit perfectly captured the spirit of the places he visited. Influenced by Nash, Beardsley, Cézanne and Picasso, he also designed and executed murals for the liner SS Orcades and for the Lion and the Unicorn Pavilion at the Festival of Britain. His illustration clients were many and include Shell London Transport and Penguin books. He tends to draw in pen and ink with washes on non-absorbent paper. He is also a highly accomplished water colourist and won the Francis Williams Book Illustration Award in 1977 and 1982.

He taught design and book illustration for many years, first at Goldsmith's College and later at the Royal College of Art, and since 1951 was a trustee of the Tate Gallery, where his work is represented. In 1956 he was made a Royal Academician.

1 *POSTER:* LONDON
TRANSPORT
DATE: 1952

2 *POSTER:* LONDON
UNDERGROUND
DATE: c. 1950

3 *BOOK:* LIFE IN AN ENGLISH
VILLAGE
DATE: 1949

1

2

3

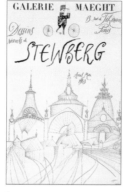

1

2

Born in Ramnic Sarat, Romania. Studied psychology and sociology at Bucharest University and in 1942 moved to Milan, where he studied architecture. In 1951 he emigrated to America and joined the staff of New Yorker magazine. During the war he served with the US Navy and then returned to New York, where he has lived ever since. He is a prolific artist, well known for his witty cartoons, or "graphic parodies", as they have been called. His illustrated books included All in Line (1945), The Art of Living (1945), The Passport (1954) and The Labyrinth (1961). An enormously influential artist, his reputation was international and he had exhibitions at the Museum of Modern Art, New York, the ICA, London, and in Paris and Amsterdam.

1 EXHIBITION POSTER
DATE: 1953

2 EXHIBITION POSTER
DATE: 1953

3 MAGAZINE: VOGUE
DATE: 1951

3

Born in Burma. Studied at Birmingham School of Art. After World War I he joined a commercial studio and also worked as a freelance illustrator. In 1936 he took over the Rupert Bear strip in the Daily Express *from its original illustrator, Mary Tourtel (1897-1940), and subsequently was identified with Rupert until his retirement in 1965, when he left a great deal of material still to be published. As well as the newspaper strip, Rupert was published in annuals, the first in 1936; at the height of their popularity during the 40s and 50s, they sold over a million and a half copies a year. Bestall followed the graphic style developed by Tourtel but introduced more humour and action into the storylines, sometimes developing a slightly surreal element to the adventures of the intrepid bear and his playmates.*

1, 2 *BOOK:* DAILY EXPRESS
ANNUAL
DATE: 1956

1

2

1

2

3

Born in Scotland. Attended life classes at Manchester Art School, then studied art at Reading University. In 1917 she moved to London, where she attended the Central School of Art and Crafts while designing book jackets and posters and illustrating children's stories. She is most famous for her Orlando books, a series of stories based on the adventures of a large marmalade cat, which she wrote for her own children. Although his adventures were flights of fantasy, the character of Orlando, like that of Jean de Brunhoff's Babar (of which Hale was a great admirer), remains perfectly plausible – in keeping with her belief that fantasy should always have some basis in reality. She was awarded the OBE in 1976.

1 *BOOK:* ORLANDO BUYS A COTTAGE *by Kathleen Hale DATE:* 1963

2, 3 *BOOK:* ORLANDO: THE FRISKY HOUSEWIFE *by Kathleen Hale DATE:* 1956

PETER BLAKE
(b. 1932)

Born in Dartford, UK. Studied
at Gravesend Technical
College and School of Art, and
attended the Royal College of
Art from 1953-56. He spent
a year studying folk art in
Europe, an experience clearly
reflected in his early work.
Other influences have been the
popular Victorian realists and
American Symbolic Realists
such as Ben Shahn. Although a
brilliant draughtsman, he was
best known during the 60s for
his collage work, incorporating
everyday consumer items,
advertisements, photographs
of pin-up girls and other
ephemera, and was very much
part of the British Pop Art
movement. His illustrative work
includes Summer with Monica by
Roger McGough, several covers
for the Arden Shakespeare series
published by Methuen, album
sleeves, posters and magazines.
He has held several one-man
exhibitions in London, Europe
and Japan, exhibited with
"The Ruralists" in 1981 and
is represented in major public
collections throughout the
world.

1

1 RECORD ALBUM COVER: SGT
PEPPER'S LONELY HEARTS
CLUB BAND
DATE: 1967

2 PERIODICAL: THE TIMES
LITERARY SUPPLEMENT
DATE: 1966

3 MAGAZINE: THE SUNDAY
TIMES MAGAZINE
DATE: 1969

2

3

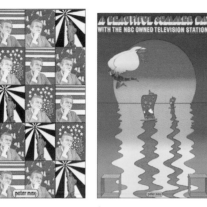

1

2

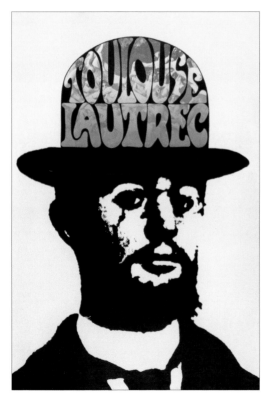

3

Born in Berlin, Germany. Spent his childhood in Shanghai, where he developed his interest in Eastern art and philosophy. When he was 12 his family moved to Israel, where he studied art and astronomy. In the mid-50s his family took him to New York, where he attended the Art Students League, the Pratt Institute and the School of Visual Arts. In 1962 he set up a design studio with his friend Daly, which over the next two years won an astonishing 68 awards for excellence in illustration, design and typography. Max's personal art form, "Cosmic Art", took its inspiration from nature as he believed that "it is in nature that the most beautiful things are to be found". Religion, mythology and oriental symbolism are all important components of his designs, which have come to epitomize the aesthetics of the 1960s.

1 *POSTER:* USA LIBERAL PARTY, NEW YORK
DATE: 1969

2 *POSTER:* NBC TELEVISION
DATE: 1969

3 *POSTER:* TOULOUSE-LAUTREC
DATE: 1967

DR SEUSS
(1904- 1991)

Born Theodor Seuss Geisel in Massachusetts, USA. He was educated at Dartmouth College and did a post-graduate year at Oxford University in England. His intention was to become a professor of English Literature. However, after travelling in Europe for a year he returned to America, where he spent 15 years working in advertising. In 1937 he published his first book, And to think that I saw it on Mulberry Street, *and published 27 children's books featuring strange creatures of his own design – hybrids of cats, bears and human beings. This strange menagerie has proven to be enduringly popular.*

1,2 *BOOK:* THE SLEEP BOOK *by Dr Seuss*
DATE: 1962

3 *BOOK:* THE FOOT BOOK *by Dr Seuss*
DATE: 1968

1

2

Left foot
Left foot

Right foot
Right

3

Born in Penistone, UK. After abandoning a promising career in chemistry, he studied at the Barnsley School of Art and then at the Slade School of Fine Art. He became a freelance illustrator at the age of 27 and had two books published in 1959, The Story of Jesus *by Eleanor Graham and* The Daffodil Bird *by Ruth Tomalin. Since then he has written and illustrated nearly 20 books, including* Brian Wildsmith's ABC, *which won the Kate Greenaway Medal in 1962. Within each of his drawings, both black and white and full colour, he uses a wide variety of media and techniques to create a striking array of textures, and his style was extremely influential throughout the 1960s.*

1

1-2 *BOOK:* BRIAN WILDSMITH'S ABC
DATE; 1962

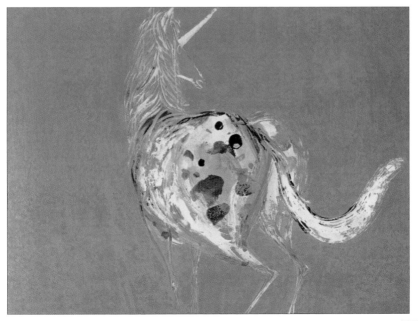

2

MARTIN SHARP
(b. 1942)

Born in Sydney, Australia. He studied at the East Sydney Art School and after graduating in 1963 produced cartoons and graphics for Richard Neville's magazine Oz. In 1966 these illustrations were published under the title Martin Sharp Cartoons and in the same year, he, Neville and Oz moved to London. Over the next three years Sharps psychedelic, day-glo paintings became icons of underground art and, as well as working prolifically for Oz, he produced posters for the Big O poster company and illustrated album covers for The Creams' Disraeli Gears and Wheels of Fire. In 1969 he returned to Australia and has since concentrated on paintings and posters. In 1972 he published Artbook, a collection of his work which reveals such diverse influences as Rene Magritte and Vincent van Gogh. He spent ten years making a film about the life of Tiny Tim, "Street of Dreams". In 1988 he exhibited his posters in Brighton, UK.

1   2

1 *MAGAZINE:* OZ
DATE: 1968

2 *MAGAZINE:* OZ
DATE: 1968

3 *POSTER:* BOB DYLAN
DATE: 1967

3

1

Born in Spain. Moscoso lives and works in America, where during the 1960s he achieved eminence as an underground artist. His earliest works were a series of posters in 1967 for the Avalon and Fillmore ballrooms in San Francisco, where bands such as the Grateful Dead were playing. In the late 1960s he was a staff artist on Rolling Stone *magazine, then in the 1970s became more involved in comic book illustration. His work appears in* All Stars *(1970), his own book* Colour *(1971), and Sci-Fi comics which also featured the drawings of Robert Crumb and Gilbert Shelton. His most notable comic work is featured in the Zap Comix series, which is still in print. Moscoso's definitively psychedelic style made him popular with underground publications around the world and he was featured heavily in London's* Oz *and* International Times. *His pictures have also appeared in* Playboy *and in advertisements for Levi jeans.*

1 *COMIC:* ZAP
DATE: c. 1969

JOHN BURNINGHAM
(b. 1936)

Born in Farnham, UK. Studied at the Central School of Art. After graduation, he wrote his own stories to get his work published. His first book, Borka: The Adventures of a Goose with no Feathers, *won the Kate Greenaway Medal in 1963, and* Mr Gumpy's Outing *won the medal again in 1970 as well as the* Boston Globe Horn Book Award *for illustration in 1972. Burningham works in full colour using an array of media – india ink crayons, gouache, cellulose, montage, printer's ink, pastel and photostats. He says of children's illustration: "A beautiful picture is not enough; a mixture of action, detail and atmosphere is important". He lives and works in London.*

1

2

1 *POSTER:* LONDON TRANSPORT
DATE: 1963

2 *POSTER:* LONDON TRANSPORT

DATE: c. 1960

3 *BOOK:* MR GUMPY'S OUTING
by John Burningham
DATE: 1970

4 *BOOK:* TROUBLOFF *by John Burningham*
DATE: 1964

3

4

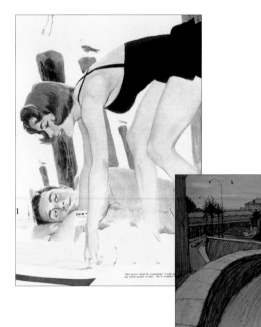

1

2

3

Born in St Louis, USA. He paid his way through art school by playing saxophone in a jazz band. On graduating he worked in a small local studio, then moved to New York in the mid-1930s. He was an immediate success and much emulated by contemporary illustrators. His extraordinary versatility was such that he once illustrated an entire issue of Cosmopolitan magazine using a different name and style for each story. He is in no way limited by technique and works comfortably in any combination of media. In 1939 he illustrated a mother-daughter cover for Ladies' Home Journal which was so popular that he completed a series of 50 of them over the next 12 years. He has won more than 25 Gold Medals for the excellence of his work and was elected to the Society of Illustrators Hall of Fame in 1965.

1 *MAGAZINE:* WOMAN
DATE: 1960

2 *MAGAZINE:* SPORTS
ILLUSTRATED
DATE: 1964

3 *ADVERTISEMENT:* AMERICAN
AIRLINES
DATE: 1965

MICHAEL ENGLISH
(b. 1943)

Born in London. *Studied at Ealing College of Art. In 1967 he formed a design company, Haphash and the Coloured Coat, with Nigel Waymouth, the co-owner of the cult King's Road shop Cranny Takes a Trip. Over the next two years they produced many psychedelic posters advertising underground events in London. English's work also appeared in the counter-culture's foremost magazine* International Times. *His paintings, which are definitive of the psychedelic era, were the product of an extraordinarily eclectic style. His influences embraced the Nouveau period of Beardsley and Mucha, Art Deco, Hindu symbolism, Japanese and Islamic decoration, Surrealist imagery and cartoon-style typography. English was also interested in the ephemera of the late 60s, designing T-shirts and sunglasses decorated with the Union Jack. With the arrival of the 70s his work changed dramatically and he abandoned the esoteric in favour of an exploration of the minutiae of urban life through his airbrushed hyper-realistic illustrations.*

1 *POSTER:* LIVERPOOL LOVE
FESTIVAL
DATE: 1968

2 *POSTER:* LOVE ME FILM
PRODUCTIONS
DJTE: 1969

3 *POSTER:* JIMI HENDRIX
CONCERT
DATE: 1968

1

2

3

1

2

Born in Philadelphia, USA. He started drawing cartoons as a child and drew comic books with his brother as a teenager. This is when he first created "Fritz the Cat", the cartoon character for which he is most famous and which was made into an X-rated animation film in 1971. In 1962 he moved to Cleveland Ohio, and, from 1964, started drawing for the underground newspapers Yarrowstalks *and* East Village Other. *In 1966 he moved to San Francisco, where he started the hugely popular Zap and* Snatch *comics. His fluid expressive cartoons, executed in pen and ink, brilliantly reflected the hippy drug culture of the 60s and early 70s, when his "Schuman the Human" and "Mr Natural" characters, and his sexually explicit cartoons, often starring himself as the unlikely victim of sex-starved women, reached the peak of their popularity. Books include* The Snatch Sampler *(1977) and* Head Comix *(1968).*

---

1 *COMIC:* NOTE
DATE: 1959

---

2 *COMIC:* ARCADE
DATE: 1962

---

3 *COMIC:* FRITZ THE CAT
DATE: 1962

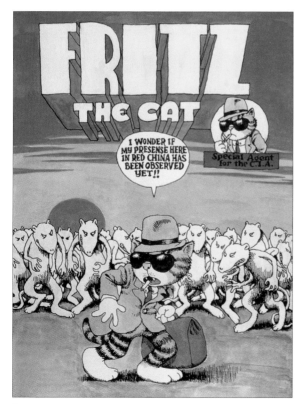

3

ROBIN JACQUES
1920- 1995)

Born in London. Brother of the actress Hattie Jacques, he was educated in Hertfordshire and worked in an advertising agency while submitting illustrations to the Radio Times. *After the war he became a full-time freelance illustrator, his first commissions being Dickens'* Doctor Marigold *(1945) and Cross's* The Angry Planet *(1945). In 1948 he was appointed art editor of* The Strand Magazine *and contributed to many other magazines, including* The Leader, The Listener, Punch, Vogue, The Sunday Times, Nova *and* The Observer. *His drawings were meticulously detailed and usually executed in line, sometimes with an ink or watercolour wash. He had a particular interest in 19th-century literature and placed a great emphasis on research to ensure the accuracy of his drawings.*

1 *MAGAZINE:* THE LEADER
DATE: 1950

2 *MAGAZINE:* THE LEADER
DATE: 1950

3 *MAGAZINE:* THE LEADER
DATE: 1950

4 *BOOK:* FORTY-TWO STORIES
by Hans Christian Andersen
DATE: 1953

1

3

2

4

1

2

3

*Born in Newcastle, UK.
Educated at King Edward VI
College in Newcastle, he went
on to study at the Royal College
of Art, London. On returning
from a travelling scholarship
to Europe, he became a teacher
at the Royal College, designing
advertising posters in his
spare time. He joined the staff
of S H Benson Ltd in 1925 and
began a long and distinguished
career in advertising art. His
posters for Guinness beer,
stylized but realistic humorous
images with accompanying
slogans such as the famous "My
goodness, my Guinness", were
produced prolifically during
the 1930s, when new ideas
were required continuously. He
also contributed illustrations
to* Radio Times *throughout
the 1930s. After World War II,
Gilroy concentrated seriously
on portrait painting working
on commissions that included
portraits of Sir Winston
Churchill as well as several
members of the British Royal
Family.*

1 *ADVERTISEMENT:*
GUINNESS BEER
DATE: 1940

2 *ADVERTISEMENT:*
GUINNESS BEER
DATE: 1956

3 *ADVERTISEMENT:*
GUINNESS BEER
DATE: 1953

BRUCE BOMBERGER
(1918-1980)

Born in California. With the exception of one year in New York, Bomberger spent his life and varied career on the West Coast of America. He started work in an art studio and at one point had a studio of his own, but eventually returned to freelancing. He worked for many different advertising clients, his most notable work being his wildlife drawings for the Weyerhaeuser Timber Company. His drawings also illustrated the stories and the editorial pages of such magazines as True, The Saturday Evening Post, Cosmopolitan, Good Housekeeping *and* This Week. *He was at one time President of the San Francisco Society of Illustrators.*

1 *PAINTING*
DATE: 1962

2 *MAGAZINE:* THE SATURDAY
EVENING POST
DATE: 1954

1

2

1

2

Born in London. Studied at London art schools before taking up a career as a freelance illustrator. He was particularly associated with The London Illustrated News *and also worked for* The Graphic *and* Radio Times. *His illustrations were typically line or line and wash but he was also an accomplished oil painter and water colourist and was elected Royal Academician in 1952. His lively approach to literary themes is exemplified by illustrations to Wycherley's* The Country Wife *(1934), conceived as scenes on stage with a strong sense of movement and dramatic lighting. He brought a fresh character to Dickens' classic* Nicholas Nickleby *(1940), but was equally attuned to the work of contemporary novelists, as in* The Circus is Coming *(1938) by Noel Streatfield and* The Valley of Song *(1951) by Elizabeth Goudge.*

1 *MAGAZINE:* THE LEADER
DATE: 1950

2 *MAGAZINE:* THE LEADER
DATE: 1950

Born in Denver, Colorado, USA. Studied geology at Wichita State University, then enrolled at the Art Centre College of Design in Los Angeles. In 1953 he moved to New York, where he was much in demand due to his ability to work in a broad range of styles using different media and techniques. His first cinema poster was for West Side Story *in 1960; since then he has illustrated posters for many box office successes, including* Camelot, *for which he won a Society of Illustrators gold medal,* Hair, The Missouri Breaks *and* The Last Emperor. *Although he denied having a particular style, he admitted to being influenced by Art Nouveau and had a passion for Egon Schiele, Degas, Matisse and the French Impressionists. His clients included* Life, Look, Esquire, Cosmopolitan, Sports Illustrated *and* Playboy *magazines, Coca Cola, the US Postal Service and a number of major film companies, including MGM and Walt Disney. He won numerous gold and silver medals, was voted Artist of the Year in 1961 by the Artists Guild of New York, won the Hamilton King Award in 1968 and was elected to the Society of Illustrators Hall of Fame in 1977.*

1   2

1 *ADVERTISEMENT.* NEW YORK WORLD'S FAIR
DATE: 1964

2 *ADVERTISEMENT:* NEWSWEEK MAGAZINE
DATE: 1964

3 *ADVERTISEMENT:* SS FRANCE
DATE: 1964

3

1

2

3

Born in Kettering, UK. Bellamy was one of the first Englishmen working in comic books to achieve international recognition as an illustrator. In the early 1950s he drew advertising campaigns for The Daily Telegraph, World's Press Agency *and* Ad Weekly *as well as illustrations for* Home Notes, Boy's Own Paper, Men Only *and covers for* Lilliput. *His first comic strip was an advertisement for a toothpaste company and was called* Commando Gibbs v Dragon Decay. *In 1957 he joined the* Eagle *comic and illustrated the life of Winston Churchill in a strip called* The Happy Warrior. *It was the first time that the biography of a living individual had been drawn in this style and it was serialized on the back page. In 1960 he was asked to redesign* Dan Dare *for the front page and in 1962 he created* Heros The Spartan, *which won him the Academy of Comic Book Arts award in America as Best Foreign Comic-Book Artist. He was an immaculate draughtsman whose work had an almost photographic realism. He inked directly onto the art board and coloured in with gouache and waterproof inks, creating artwork that was as perfect as the printed page. In the latter part of his life he gave up comics, but continued to draw a black-and-white newspaper strip called* Garth *until his death in 1976.*

1 *MAGAZINE:* EAGLE
DATE: 1960

2 *MAGAZINE:* EAGLE
DATE: 1960

3 *MAGAZINE:* EAGLE
DATE: 1963

BRIAN LOVE
(b. 1942)

Born in London. Studied at
Gravesend and Walthamstow
Schools of Art and the Royal
College of Art. From the mid-60s
his obsession with American and
British popular culture, and his
collection of popular magazines
and juvenile literature, became
the prime source of reference
for his illustration work, much
of which attempted to pastiche
the colour and compositional
arrangement found in such
publications. His work as a
print maker greatly influenced
the way in which he assembled
and designed his illustrations.
In many cases he produced line-
separated artwork which only
formed the completed image when
printed. His work has appeared
in Town, Nova, Radio Times, The
Sunday Times, Observer and
Vogue magazines and illustrated
The Beatles' Lyrics in 1968. Even
more prolific as a fine artist, he
has had one-man exhibitions of
his sculptures in Holland and
Germany. In 1978 he mounted a
touring exhibition entitled Aerial
Drop" – a never-before-seen
collection of propaganda leaflets
dropped from airplanes. He has
also compiled two books on board
games, Play the Game (1978) and
Great Board Games (1979).

1

1 *MAGAZINE:* RADIO TIMES
DATE: 1969

2 *MAGAZINE:* THE SUNDAY
TIMES MAGAZINE
DATE: 1969

3 *MAGAZINE:* THE SUNDAY
TIMES MAGAZINE
DATE: 1969

2

3

4

5

4 *AIRBRUSHED BLACK AND WHITE PHOTOGRAPH:* DAVID BAILEY AND MARIE HELVIN *(unpublished)* *DATE.* 1969

5 *MAGAZINE:* THE SUNDAY TIMES MAGAZINE *DATE:* 1969

6 *MAGAZINE:* THE SUNDAY TIMES MAGAZINE *DATE:* 1968

6

Born in London. Trained as a typographer at the London College of Printing and then worked as assistant to Hans Neuberg. In 1965 he became a freelance illustrator and graphic designer and over the next four years worked regularly for magazines such as The Sunday Times and Radio Times. In 1969 he moved to America and from 1970-75 was art director of Esquire magazine. He received numerous awards for his work which he says was never inspired by other illustrators but by the films, pop and montage art of the time. From 1975-79 he was director of the Children's Television Workshop, an educational development of the Sesame Street Muppets. He still lives and works in New York where he is freelance consultant and planner to the magazine publishing industry.

1 *MAGAZINE:* THE SUNDAY TIMES MAGAZINE
DATE: 1968

2 *MAGAZINE:* THE SUNDAY TIMES MAGAZINE
DATE: 1968

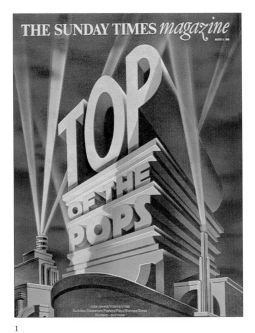

1

2

1

2

3

Born near Cambridge, UK. Studied at Cambridge School of Art, where he met Peter Fluck, with whom he later formed the partnership responsible for the Spitting Image TV series. After leaving college he worked with Peter Cook on a satirical strip for the Observer, and also drew giant topical cartoons for the walls of Cook's nightclub The Establishment where he met Lenny Bruce and other stand-up comics who influenced his later work. In 1963 he joined the art department of The Sunday Times magazine as an illustrator and collaborated with David King on a series of record covers and posters. In 1967 he was a Rockefeller Foundation winner, was artist-in-residence at Reed College, Oregon, for six months and spent the following two years in America. He did fashion drawings and illustration in San Francisco and worked at Push Pin Studios in New York. On his return to England he became features editor of The Sunday Times magazine and in 1975 formed the Luck and Flaw partnership with Peter Fluck. Together they created the hit British comedy TV show, Spitting Image.

1 *MAGAZINE:* THE SUNDAY TIMES MAGAZINE
DATE: c. 1968

2 *MAGAZINE:* THE SUNDAY TIMES MAGAZINE
DATE. 1969

3 *MAGAZINE:* NOVA
DATE: c. 1967

Born in Detroit, Michigan, USA. Studied at the Wicker Art School. He began his art career as assistant to an automobile illustrator, then drew for the Dearborn Independent before enrolling at the Art Students League in New York. During the Depression he did a variety of jobs, including ghosting the Flash Gordon strip and doing pulp illustrations for Blue Book *magazine. He had an unlimited repertoire of techniques, sometimes reducing his drawings to the barest line and at other times illustrating in delicate coloured washes. Most prolific at a time when photography was making real inroads into magazine publishing he specialized in the candid pose, mimicking the camera's ability to freeze the moment, and often seeming to catch his subject unawares. His work appeared in* Collier's, McClure's, Cosmopolitan, Redbook *and* The Saturday Evening Post, *and his advertising clients included Douglas PC Airliners. He was elected to the Society of Illustrators Hall of Fame in 1969.*

1

1 *MAGAZINE:* WOMAN
DATE: 1960

1

2

Born in London. The son of a keen amateur artist, he grew up in Canada and New York. At the age of 19 he returned to London to study at the Slade School of Fine Art, then in 1924 returned to America and embarked on a career as a freelance illustrator. His superb draughtsmanship and compositions quickly earned him a reputation as one of America's finest illustrators, and he worked prolifically on editorial and advertising commissions. During the 1950s he limited his work to reportage and in 1958 he wrote and illustrated On the Art of Drawing. *He returned to London in 1960 to paint a series of murals for the Commonwealth Institute and in 1967 was elected to the Society of Illustrators Hall of Fame.*

1. *MAGAZINE:* COLLIER'S
DATE: 1951

2 *MAGAZINE:* COLLIER'S
DATE: 1951

3 *MAGAZINE:* THE SATURDAY
EVENING POST
DATE: 1945

3

ROWLAND EMETT
(1906-1995)

Born in London. Trained at Birmingham College of Arts and Crafts. Emett was known as the latter-day Heath Robinson, both for his graphic work and for his working models of the eccentric machines described in his illustrations. His fascination for railways was seen in twelve books produced between 1943 and 1958, including Engines, Aunties and Others *(1943),* Sidings and Suchlike *(1946) and* Buffer's End *(1949). His figures frequently seemed as endearingly antiquated as his machines. He contributed illustrations to* Punch, Life, Vogue *and* Harper's Bazaar, *among others, and created advertising images for Shell and Guinness. He converted antique railway drawings into a full-size, passenger-carrying model for the Festival of Britain in 1951, and produced the Edwardian-style vehicles featured in the 1968 film* Chitty Chitty Bang Bang. *He created smaller models for window displays and commercial exhibitions.*

1-4 *BOOK:* BELLS AND GRASS
by Walter De La Mare
DATE: 1941

1

2

3

4

1

*Born in London. Studied at
Westminster School of Art
under Walter Sickert, then at
Goldsmith's School of Art, where
he was influenced by the line
draughtsman Edmund Sullivan
and the painter Clive Gardiner.
In 1924 he exhibited etchings
at the Royal Academy and from
1930-38 was a fashion designer
for* Harper's Bazaar. *Although
perhaps best remembered for
the strong black and white
illustrations he produced for
the BBC, and which appeared
frequently in the* Radio Times,
*he was also a stained glass
artist and designed murals for
the Glasgow Exhibition in 1938
and the Festival of Britain in
1951. He taught lithography at
Goldsmith's and graphic design
at Camberwell School of Art and
his illustrated books include*
English Legends *(1951),* The
Book of a Thousand and One
Nights *(1958) and* Sir William
and the Wolf *(1960).*

1 *MAGAZINE:* RADIO TIMES
DATE. c. 1940

2 *MAGAZINE:* RADIO TIMES
DATE: c. 1940

3 *MAGAZINE:* RADIO TIMES
DATE: c. 1940

2

3

CHAPTER FOUR

OVER THE LAST 150 YEARS politics and war have created an important field of activity for the illustrator. However, the period since 1970 has been one of relative stability, and the ensuing prosperity in the West has had a subtle but profound effect on artists' lives.

The psychedelic '60s actually ended in about 1972, by which time most of their excesses had been softened by their absorption into mainstream culture. The next style revolution was that of punk rock, which took place about three years later. Its effect was most noticeable in the worlds of fashion and music, but it did make an impact on graphic design and particularly on typography. Its effect on illustration was less noticeable. The '60s had enabled illustrators to develop such a diversity of styles that there was nao predominant school for punk aestheticism to assail and therefore no obvious reaction took place.

The main influences on illustration have in fact come from developments within the publishing industry. It is a common belief that book illustration went into decline during the period between the wars and that it has never recovered. This is not entirely true. One has only to look through the examples in this chapter to see that children's book illustration is still booming in the hands of such artists as Helen Oxenbury, Wayne Anderson, Nicola Bayley and Michael Foreman. In fact this market is so healthy that many illustrators, like Maurice Sendak in the USA, have taken to writing their own stories as opposed to reinterpreting the commercial classics. An interesting consequence of this has been the opportunity for artists such as Raymond Briggs to then diversify into animation by selling story rights to a film company.

What has changed is the range of activities within book publishing. The gift book, in the Edwardian sense, has all but disappeared. Modern novels and poetry are rarely illustrated. The craze for coffee-table books has focused on popular education subjects that have been best documented by photography.

However, the book industry as a whole continues to expand and provide a plentiful supply of work in the form of paperback covers and dust jackets. And, perhaps to carve a niche within this market, it seems increasingly common for illustrators to specialize within a literary genre. This is particularly true of science fiction, a field which is now dominated by the styles of artists like Jim Burns, Chris Foss and Peter Jones.

As far as the illustrator is concerned, the magazine business has never been so promising. Prosperity creates increased leisure time and with it the proliferation of special interest magazines. These in turn create interesting possibilities for younger artists: as production budgets are often low while a magazine struggles to establish itself, and consequently art departments are prepared to experiment with less proven, but less expensive talent.

Advertising, too, is going from strength to strength, and provides artists with a major source of work. It also encourages a diversity of styles, as the very nature of its business is to differentiate, both practically and aesthetically, one product from another. This has led many illustrators to find work at the agencies and, because advertising is the most plagiaristic of skills, it has proven especially lucrative for artists, like Mick Brownfield in the UK, who can accurately parody bygone styles.

The current diversity of media opportunities has led to a correspondingly wide range of illustration styles. But no real "stars" have emerged. Illustrators, unlike their counterparts of the '20s, are no longer household names. The artist Bernie Fuchs said in his introduction to a book on American illustration that the illustrator today is more like a businessman than the artist of old. But if that's the case, one has to say that business is good.

CHAPTER FOUR

ROGER DEAN
(b. 1944)

*Born in Kent, UK. Studied
industrial design (furniture)
at the Canterbury School of
Art (1961-64), then spent three
years at the Royal College of
Art. His first assignment was to
design the seating for "Upstairs"
at Ronnie Scott's jazz club in
London. Between 1968 and 1973
he worked prolifically, designing
stage sets, posters, furniture,
hotels and office towers. His
record-sleeve designs for the
rock groups Osibisa, Yes, Asia
and the Rolling Stones quickly
established him as the foremost
illustrator of record-album
covers in Britain. With his
brother, Martyn, he formed the
company Dragon's Dream in
1975 to publish his book* Views,
*featuring Roger's fantasy and
science fiction designs for record
sleeves. Packed with hundreds
of colour plates, and selling for
the price of a record album, it
went straight to the top of* The
Sunday Times *best-seller list
and sold half a million copies
world-wide. In 1976 the Deans
set up a second company, with
Hubert Schaafsma, to publish
books under the Paper Tiger
imprint. In 1979 he became a
director of the Magnetic Storm
design company, specializing
in product research and
development. He is currently
working on a film, "Floating
Islands" which will feature
animated 3D renderings of his
classic images.*

1

2

3

4

5

MAURICE SENDAK
(b. 1928)

Born in Brooklyn, New York. Studied at the Art Students League. In 1952 he illustrated A Hole is to Dig *by Ruth Krauss. It was a huge success, and revolutionary in its day because there was no storyline; the book consisted of a series of illustrated children s definitions, such as "dogs are to kiss people", and so on. Although Sendak's illustrations appeared in many books by other authors, his most significant books were those he wrote himself, including* Where the Wild Things Are (1962), *which won both the Hans Christian Andersen and the Caldecott awards,* In the Night Kitchen (1970) *and* Higglety Pigglety Pop! (1967), *which was written in dedication to his dog, Julie, who had died shortly before. Increasingly Sendak has begun to link his art to music. He co-wrote, with Carole King, an animated TV musical* Really Rosie, *and wrote the libretto and designed the sets for an opera version of* Where the Wild Things Are *in 1979 and later worked on children's opera* Brundibar *in 2003. A film version of* Where the Wild Things Are *is planned for 2008.*

1-2 BOOK: WHERE THE WILD THINGS ARE *by Maurice Sendak* DATE: 1962

2 BOOK INTHENIGHT KITCHEN *by Maurice Sendak* DATE: 1970

1

2

3

1

Born in Singapore. Studied graphic design at Saint Martin's School of Art and then entered the Royal College of Art, where she studied illustration and developed a style that is rich in detail and colour and which uses a fine stippling technique to create a range of distinctive textures. Her illustrations of old nursery rhymes were spotted by a publisher in her diploma show and were later published in a book, One Old Oxford Ox (1976). She followed this with Nicola Bayley's Book of Nursery Rhymes and Richard Adams' The Tyger Voyage (both 1976), and The Patchwork Cat (1981). All were extremely successful and have been translated into seven languages. She lives in London and works in Arthur Rackham's old studio. She is currently working on The Moglie Stories, taken from The Jungle Book.

1, 2 BOOK: ONE OLD OXFORD OX by Nicola Bayley
DATE: 1977

3, 4 BOOK: THE TYGER VOYAGE by Nicola Bayley & Richard Adams
DATE: 1976

2

3

4

QUENTIN BLAKE
(b. 1932)

Born in Sidcup, UK. Studied at Downing College, Cambridge, London University and Chelsea College of Art. He began drawing for Punch *while still at school, and after leaving university also became a regular cover artist for* The Spectator *and designed book jackets for Penguin Books. His first illustrations for children's books appeared in 1960, since when he has illustrated over 150 books, most of them for children, and has had extended collaborations with Roald Dahl, Russell Hoban, Joan Aiken, Michael Rosen and John Yeoman. His* How Tom Beat Captain Najork and his Hired Sportsmen *was joint winner of the Whitbread Award (1974) and* Mister Magnolia *won the Kate Greenaway Medal (1980). He is now a visiting professor at the Royal College of Art, of which he is a Senior Fellow, and where he was Head of Illustration between 1978 and 1986. He was awarded the OBE in 1988. He was appointed Children's Laureate of Great Britain in 1999, and received the international Han's Christian Anderson Award for Illustration in 2002.*

1 *BOOK:* RUMBELOW'S DANCE *by John Yeoman*
DATE: 1982

2 *MAGAZINE:* PUNCH
DATE: 1980

3 *BOOK:* A FEAST OF TRUE FANDANGLES *by Patrick Campbell*
DATE: 1979

4 *BOOK:* THE BIRDS *by Aristophanes*
DATE: 1971

5 *BOOK:* THE HISTORY OF TOM THUMB
DATE: 1979

1

2

3

4

5

1

2

3

Born in London. Studied at St Albans School of Art and the Royal College of Art, where he taught for two years. Since 1955 he has concentrated on his own work, which has included lithography, wood-engraving, graphic design and watercolour painting and ranges in scale from postage stamps to the platform-length murals on the Underground at Charing Cross station in London. Publishing clients include Penguin Books, Cambridge University Press, Limited Editions Club of New York, Cape and Weidenfeld. He has produced several books of his own, including David Gentleman's Britain *(1982),* David Gentleman's London *(1985),* David Gentleman's Coastline *(1988),* A Special Relationship *(1987) and, with Russell Hoban,* The Dancing Tigers *(1979). He has also written and illustrated several children's books and one book on design.*

1 *BOOK:* A MIDSUMMER NIGHT'S DREAM *by William Shakespeare*
DATE: 1975

2 *BOOK:* HENRY VIII *by William Shakespeare*
DATE: 1975

3 *BOOK:* THE DANCING TIGERS *by David Gentleman & Russell Hoban*
DATE: 1979

BRUCE PENNINGTON
(b. 1944)

Born in Somerset, UK. Studied at
Beckenham and Ravensbourne
Schools of Art in Kent. After
graduating in 1964 he worked
for two years as a commercial
artist before becoming a
freelance illustrator in 1967,
entering the science fiction field
with his cover design for Robert
Heinlein's Stranger in a Strange
Land. This marked a turning
point in his career and, finding
science-fiction an excellent
medium through which to
express his imaginative ideas,
he went on to produce covers for
several Ray Bradbury novels for
Corgi Books. Many of his works
were reproduced in Science
Fiction Monthly.

1-3 *BOOK:* ESCHATUS *by Bruce*
Pennington
DATE: 1917

1

2

3

1

*Born in London. Studied at
Saint Martin's School of Art,
where, inspired by the novels
of Isaac Asimov and Larry
Niven, he became interested
in science fiction imagery. His
freelance career took off while
he was still at college, with some
commissions for Puffin Books.
In 1979 he designed a book,
Solar Wind, with Roger and
Martyn Dean. In the same year,
Solar Wind Ltd was formed
to market his career, and he
branched out into film, TV and
video productions. In 1982 he
launched a highly successful
series of Fighting Fantasy games
books for Puffin. He has also
designed news title sequences,
backdrops and inserts for BBC
Television, and has exhibited in
England, France and Japan.*

1 *BOOK:* THE QUEST OF THE
DNA COWBOYS *by Mick Farren*
DATE: 1975

2 *BOOK:* THE COMPLETE
ENCHANTER *by L Sprague de
Camp and Fletcher Pratt*
DATE: 1979

2

JEAN-MICHEL FOLON
(1934- 2005)

*Born in Brussels, Belgium.
Initially studied architecture,
but abandoned it in favour
of becoming an illustrator.
Since the mid-60s he produced
a vast body of work and his
wistful, poetic, watercolours,
particularly those featuring his
"blue man", appeared in many
media. He produced advertising
posters for Olivetti, film posters
for Woody Allen, and record
covers for Michele Colombier
and Steve Kahn; illustrated
the works of Kafka and Lewis
Carroll (1973),
and the short stories of Jorge-
Luis Borges (1974); created
frescoes for the Belgian metro
and the London Underground;
designed theatre scenery for
the operas of Frank Martin and
Puccini; and produced animated
films for Cadbury's chocolate
in the UK and title sequences
for French TV. In addition to
all this, he held one-man shows
around the world.*

1 *POSTER:* AMNESTY
INTERNATIONAL
DATE: 1977

2 *POSTER*
DATE: 1975

3 *POSTER*
DATE: 1977

4 *EXHIBITION POSTER*
DATE: 1977

5 *SOURCE:* NOT KNOWN
DATE: NOT KNOWN

1

1

2

3

4

JAN PIENKOWSKI
(b. 1936)

Born in Warsaw, Poland. He read English and the Classics at Cambridge and in 1961 was a co-founder of Gallery Five, a greetings card company through which many of his books have been published. In 1967 he illustrated Jessie Townsend's Annie, Bridget and Charlie *and in 1968 formed a collaboration with Joan Aiken which led three years later to the publication of* The Kingdom Under The Sea and Other Stories *(1972), which won the Kate Greenaway Medal. Since 1972 he has produced the* Meg *and* Mog *series, featuring simplified drawings using strong fat colours, and highly elaborate pop-up books such as* Haunted House *(1979), a masterpiece of paper engineering which won him the Kate Greenaway Medal for the second time. Recently he has done most of his work on computer, producing a CD Rom version of* Haunted House *in 1996, and has worked on several theatre productions.*

1, 2 *BOOK:* HAUNTED HOUSE
by Jan Pienkowski
DATE: 1979

Do you think it's all imagination? Doctor..? DOCTOR, WHERE ARE YOU..?

1

I can't seem to settle down. In fact I can't   sit still for two minutes.

2

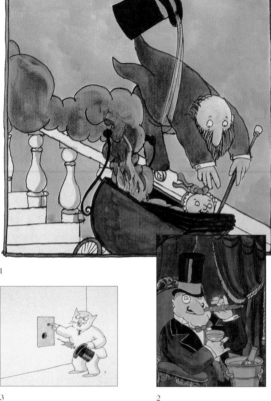

Born in Strasbourg, France.
Spent his early adulthood
travelling and doing odd jobs,
including a brief stint as a
camel-rider with the Sahara
Police Force. At the age of 24
he taught himself to draw and
paint, and in 1957 moved
to New York and established
himself as a freelance illustrator.
He was immediately successful
and his exquisite pen and
ink drawings with coloured
washes appeared in Life,
Esquire, McCalls, The New York
Times and in many advertising
campaigns. At the same time he
was writing and illustrating his
own stories and published The
Mellops Go Diving for Treasure
(1957), The Mellops Go Flying
(1957) and Emile (1960). He
won the New York Society of
Illustrators Gold Medal in 1960
and the New York Times Best
Book of the Year in 1971. Since
then he has illustrated many
books, including I am Papa Snap
and these are my favourite no-
such stories (1973), Moon Man
(1980) and The Hat (1986).

1-2 BOOK: THE HAT
DATE: 1986

3 CALENDAR DESIGN FOR
NIXDORF COMPUTERS
DATE: 1979

4 POSTER: "THE ELECTRIC
CIRCUS"
DATE: 1973

5 CALENDAR DESIGN FOR
REGENSDORF
DATE: 1979

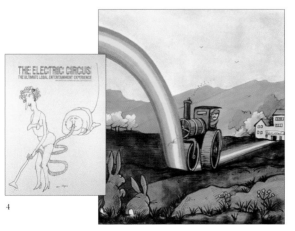

BERNARD D'ANDREA
(b. 1923)

Born in Buffalo, New York. During World War II he spent three years as a War Artist attached to the Quatermaster Corps and the Office of Strategic Services. He began his career as an illustrator in New York in 1950. His first major commission was for The Saturday Evening Post *and between 1950 and 1970 he also illustrated for* Good Housekeeping, Cosmopolitan, Ladies' Home Journal, *and* Woman's Home Companion, *as well as a number of advertising clients. Since 1970 he has concentrated more on book illustration and has worked on historical subjects for the National Geographic Society of Washington DC. He has held several one-man exhibitions and is a member of the New York Society of Illustrators.*

1 *MAGAZINE:* BOY'S LIFE
DATE: 1973

2 *BOOK:* THE MAN WHO MADE
THE BEATLES
DATE: 1976

3 *MAGAZINE:* GOOD
HOUSEKEEPING
DATE: 1976

4 *MAGAZINE:* REDBOOK
DATE: 1976

2

3

1

4

1

2

3

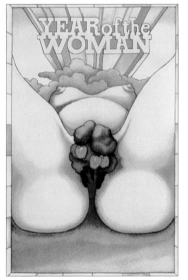

4

Born in New York. Trained at the Pratt Institute and at Hunter College. She worked briefly as a textile designer, then spent a year in Europe. On her return to America in 1963, she embarked on a career of freelance illustration. Her style, which she describes then as being one of "anthropomorphic double-images", was perfectly suited to the psychedelic period of the mid to late 60s, and after the publication of her poster for the "Electric Circus" she received many commissions from magazines and advertising clients. Using concentrated watercolour, ink and coloured pencils on watercolour paper, she produced images that were surreal graphic and intensely colourful. She is now one of the foremost water colourists working in America, has exhibited in New York, West Germany, Japan and the UK and published Watercolour for Illustration *in 1986.*

1 *ADVERTISEMENT:* SWEDISH TANNING PRODUCT
DATE: 1970

2 *MAGAZINE COVER:* SUNDAY MAGAZINE
DATE: 1971

3 *RECORD ALBUM COVER:* CHOPIN
DATE: c. 1970

4 *POSTER:* "YEAR OF THE WOMAN"
DATE: 1971

WAYNE ANDERSON
(b. 1946)

*Born in Leicester, UK. Studied
at Leicester College of Art
and then pursued a freelance
career in London, illustrating
album covers, greetings cards
and Clement Freud's cookery
column in the* Daily Telegraph.
*After marriage and the birth
of his first child he returned
to Leicester and concentrated
on finely detailed crayon and
pencil drawings of animals. His
first book,* Ratsmagic (1976),
*was a great success and others
quickly followed, including*
Magic Circus, Mouse's Tale *and
a collection of short stories,*
The Magic Inkstand, *written
by Heinrich Seidle. His one
adult book,* Flight of Dragons,
*written by Peter Dickenson,
was animated into a full-length
feature film and shown on
British and American television.*

1-3 *BOOK:* RATSMAGIC *by
Wayne Anderson
DATE: 1976*

1

2

3

1

Born in Aylesbury, UK. He left Romford Technical College at 15 and drifted through a variety of jobs, including actor, insurance clerk, barrow boy and stall holder in a London market. At the age of 20 he started to draw and took an evening class in graphic art. Success followed very quickly and soon his work was seen on book covers, album sleeves, posters and in magazines such as Harper's, Nova *and* The Sunday Times. *Within the world of music he was a celebrity artist and received many commissions from leading rock bands and his work appeared frequently in* Melody Maker. *In 1966 he became art director of Penguin Books and then set up his own studio in 1968. The following year he edited and contributed illustrations to both volumes of* The Beatles Illustrated Lyrics *(1969). To the psychedelic art of the 1960s Aldridge brought exquisite draughtsmanship and the innovative use of the airbrush to control the subtle gradation of tone and colour. And although his work was the epitome of the style and aesthetics of the time, it found a new audience when the decade was over. In 1974 he won the Children's Book of the Year Award for* The Butterfly Ball *(1973). He now works freelance in London and has recently been designing animated films.*

1-3 *BOOK:* THE BUTTERFLY BALL *by Alan Aldridge & William Plomer*
DATE: 1973

2   3

PAUL LEITH
(b. 1946)

*Born in South Shields, UK.
He studied commercial art
at Sunderland Art College
(1961—65) and attended the
London College of Printing
in 1969 before going on to
study illustration at the Royal
College of Art (1970—73).*
Magazine clients include
Vogue, The Sunday Times,
Observer, Company *and* She,
*and he has illustrated books for
Penguin, Futura, Octopus, Pan/
Picador and Mitchell Beazley.
Advertising clients include
retailers Liberty, Next and
The Body Shop, Royal Bank of
Scotland, Barclays Bank and the
construction company Costain.
He exhibited in the 1983, 1984
(when he won first prize) and
1985 Benson and Hedges Gold
Awards exhibitions. An admirer
of the Bauhaus and Russian
art, Leith favours a direct, no-
nonsense approach to his art. He
works mainly with stencils and
acrylic paint.*

1 "TIME PASSING"
*(Benson and Hedges Gold
Awards)*
BATE: 1984

2 "RELEASING ENERGY"
*(Benson and Hedges Gold
Awards)*
DATE: 1985

1

2

1

2

3

Born in New York. Studied at the Pratt Institute and the Pratt Graphic Art Centre in New York, graduating in 1960. After a brief spell as a textile designer, she returned to her childhood ambition to be an artist after befriending Robert Weaver, who gave her individual tuition and the encouragement to enter her work in the Society of Illustrators show in 1960. Since then she has received over 200 awards for excellence in fine art and illustration. She has illustrated album covers and calendars and for numerous magazines, including Show, New York Magazine, Audience, Ms, Rolling Stone, The Boston Globe, Newsweek *and* Time. *She has taken part in exhibitions all over the world and her work is represented at the Museum of Modern Art in New York, the Smithsonian Institution in Washington and Lund Kunsthall Lund in Sweden. She taught at the School of Visual Art, the Fashion Institute of Technology and the Pratt Institute in New York. Nessim employs many different expressive media in her work including computer graphics. She is currently working on commissions for lobby design in New York.*

1 *MAGAZINE:* V MAGAZINE
DATE: 1988

2 *PAINTING:* WOMAN SITTING
DATE: 1987

3 *PAINTING:* TEA LEAVES
DATE: 1989

DAVID AND RENEE STREET
(b. 1957 and 1954)

1

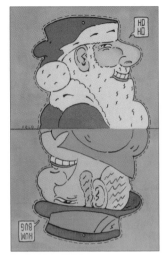

2

Renee Gettier was born in Baltimore, USA, and studied art at Towson State University before transferring to Maryland Institute, College of Fine Art. After graduating she worked as an illustrator's assistant for a year before turning freelance and starting Streetworks Studio with David Street. At various times her work has been selected as among the best of the year by Graphis, Print Magazine, The Illustrators Club *and the Art Directors Club of Metropolitan Washington. Clients include* The Washington Post, Psychology Today, 321 Contact, *McDonalds hamburger chain and CBS Records. David Street was born in Washington, USA. He studied architecture at Virginia Polytechnic and State University before transferring to Maryland Institute, College of Fine Art After starting work as a graphic designer he Joined Renee as a freelance illustrator. Clients include* The Boston Globe *and* National Wildlife Magazine. *He became President of the Illustrators Club of Washington in 1987.*

3

1 *CHILDREN'S NEWSPAPER:* PENNY WHISTLE PRESS
DATE: 1988

2 *MAGAZINE:* SCIENCE '86
DATE: 1986

3 *NEWSPAPER:* THE WASHINGTON POST
DATE: 1985

4 *CHRISTMAS CARD*
DATE: 1987

5 *NEWSPAPER:* THE BALTIMORE SUN
DATE: 1988

4

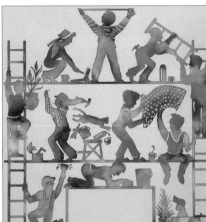

5

1

2

3

4

BILL NELSON
(b. 1946)

Born in Richmond, Virginia, USA. Graduated from the Richmond Professional Institute in 1970 with a BFA in Communication Art and Design, and began work as a newspaper illustrator on The Richmond Mercury *before setting up his own studio. His work, which has been described as "quiet elegance in coloured pencil", has appeared in* Newsweek, New Times, The Washington Post Magazine *and* Time Life *records. He has won two gold medals from the Art Directors Club of New York and two silver medals from the Society of Illustrators, who in 1983 sponsored a travelling exhibition of his work to Europe and Japan. He has lectured at a number of art schools throughout the USA and taught at The Virginia Commonwealth University's School of the Arts for two years.*

1. *BOOK:* FINISHING THE HAT. "TRENCH COAT"
DATE: 1986

2 *RECORD ALBUM COVER:* MAHLER'S SYMPHONY FOR CHILDREN
DATE: 1988

3 "AIN'T MISBEHAVIN" *(unpublished)*
DATE: 1988

1

2

3

1

RICHARD ADAMS
(b. 1960)

Born in Hampshire, UK. Studied graphic design at Leicester Polytechnic, specializing in illustration. He has won several Benson and Hedges Gold Awards prizes, including second prizes in 1983 and 1984 and first prize in 1986, and was highly commended in 1987. He also won first prize in the 1986 Reader's Digest Young Illustrators Awards. Clients include Cosmopolitan and The Listener magazines, Penguin Books, the Royal Academy of Arts, BBC World Service and a number of advertising clients. He has taken part in several group exhibitions and his work is on permanent show at the Portal Gallery in London and the David Adamson Gallery in Washington. Adams prefers to work in chalk pastel for its good tonal quality, strong colours and speed, and cites his influence as British naive art and the work of Stanley Spencer.

1 "THE JOURNEY"
(non-commissioned)
DATE: 1987

2 "THE FLORIST"
(non-commissioned)
DATE: 1989

3 "THE SHELL HOUSE AND SUN FISH"
(non-commissioned)
DATE: 1989

2

3

DAVE CALVER
(b. 1954)

Born in Rochester, New York. He graduated from Rhode Island School of Design in 1976 and immediately established himself as a freelance illustrator. His first commissions were from GQ, Psychology Today *and* New York *magazine. Initially influenced by George Grosz and the films of Fritz Lang, he works in coloured pencil and wryly observes that it is the elegance of his style that has led to his recent popularity with the publishers of murder mystery fiction. As well as illustrating book jackets he contributes regularly to* Vogue *and* Vanity Fair *and has worked for such advertising clients as Mobil, TWA and United Airlines.*

1 *BOOK JACKET:* SEDUCTION BY LIGHT
DATE: 1988

2 *MAGAZINE:* PLAYBOY
DATE: 1986

3 *POSTER:* 21ST ANNUAL COMPETITION, SOCIETY OF PUBLICATION DESIGNERS
DATE: 1986

1

2

3

1

2

3

4

5

Born in London. Trained at Hornsey College of Art and has worked as a freelance illustrator since 1973. It is difficult to characterize his work as he is not only prolific but extraordinarily versatile and has on many occasions been commissioned to parody the work of other artists, an example being his drawing for Heineken beer in the style of John Gilroy's poster for Guinness. His work has regularly appeared in the Design and Art Direction Annual, European Illustration, Association of Illustrators *exhibitions and* The One Show Annual *(New York). He has exhibited at several art galleries, including the Pompidou Centre in Paris, and has held a one-man show in Hamburg West Germany, entitled "Art for Commerce". Advertising and editorial clients include* The Sunday Times *and* Marie Claire *magazines, Guinness, Heineken, Walt Disney and Handmade Films.*

1 *MAGAZINE:* THE SUNDAY TIMES
DATE: 1987

2 *MAGAZINE:* THE LISTENER
DATE: 1984

3 *ADVERTISEMENT:*
(unpublished)
DATE: 1986

4 *MAGAZINE:* MARIE FRANCE
DATE: 1983

5 *MAGAZINE:* THE LISTENER
DATE: 1986

Roger Law (b. 1941), (see also page 233), and Peter Fluck (b 1941) met in 1957 as students at Cambridge School of Art, where they co-art directed the Cambridge University magazine Granta and were inspired by the example of their tutor, Paul Hogarth, "a man doing something he really liked and making a living". After graduating in 1963, Fluck worked as a freelance cartoonist for numerous magazines, including New Society, New Statesman, The Economist and the Radio Times, as well as designing costumes for the Royal Ballet. In 1975 the Luck and Flaw partnership was formed and produced caricature models for photography for several magazines and newspapers, illustrated Dickens' A Christmas Carol (1979) and Stevenson's Treasure Island (1986) and designed a range of ceramic caricature tableware. The Spitting Image TV series, a satirical show starring cruelly accurate caricature puppets of politicians, celebrities and members of the Royal Family, became an instant success in 1984 and led to numerous spin-offs, including books, pop songs and advertising commissions.

1-6 *TV SERIES:* SPITTING IMAGE

1 THE QUEEN *(1984)*

2 PRINCE CHARLES *(1984)*

3 FRANK BRUNO *(1985)*

4 MARGARET THATCHER *(1984)*

5 P W BOTHA *(1986)*

6 MICHAEL JACKSON *(1984)*

1

2

3

4

5

6

1

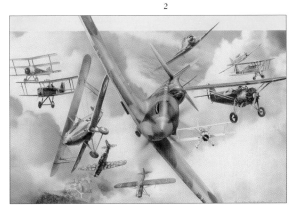

2

*Born in Huddersfield, UK.
Trained at Huddersfield School
of Art and the Royal College.
While still a student he received
his first commissions, in 1965,
from* The Sunday Times *and*
Vogue *magazines and in 1967
he was represented in an
exhibition of five illustrators
at the Time-Life Gallery. Since
then he has designed a number
of film posters, including those
for A Clockwork Orange, Full
Metal Jacket and Mars Attacks,
and worked on the 1973 Pirelli
Calendar with Allen Jones
Castle has become one of the
definitive artists of the hyper-
realistic airbrush style. He has
exhibited in San Francisco
and at the Thumb Gallery and
Francis Kyle Gallery in London.
Magazine clients include* Elle,
Marie Claire, Stern, Jasmin,
Playboy *and* Time. *Advertising
clients include Heineken,
Fiat, Ford Air Canada and
Volkswagen. He has produced
two books:* Airflow *(1980) and*
Airshow *(1989), and more
recently has designed album
covers for the band,* Pulp.

1 *FILM POSTER:* CLOCKWORK
ORANGE
DATE: 1971

2 *POSTCARD:* "TRULY
TRIONIC"
DATE: 1978

3 "PATRICK LIDSEY AIRFORCE"
(private commission)
DATE: 1983

3

GUY BILLOUT
(b. 1941)

Born in Decize, France. Studied at the Ecole des Arts Appliqués in Beaune, Burgundy. In 1969 he moved to New York, where he joined an evening art class run by Milton Glaser. This led to his entire portfolio being reprinted in New York Magazine, *of which Glaser was then editor. The idea for his first children's book,* Bus Number 24 *(1972), a picture story without words, came from a story by Heinrich Hoffman which he came across in an old German book. Since then he has produced several books for children and adults, four of which were chosen by* The New York Times *for their list of ten best-illustrated children's books. He has also illustrated for* Atlantic, New Republic, Time, Vogue, Playboy *and* Rolling Stone *magazines. Billout has received three gold and two silver medals from the Society of Illustrators, was selected as Illustrator of the Year for the All-Star Creative Team in* Adweek Creativity *(1986) and won first prize in an international contest to design a poster for the World Fair of 1992 in Seville, Spain. His intriguing, meticulously airbrushed images are influenced by Japanese woodblocks and by the flat tones of Hergé, creator of the "Tintin" comic strip.*

---

1 *MAGAZINE:* ATLANTIC
MONTHLY
DATE: 1986

---

2 *MAGAZINE:* ATLANTIC
MONTHLY
DATE: 1988

---

3 *MAGAZINE:* ATLANTIC
MONTHLY
DATE: 1987

---

4 *MAGAZINE:* CORPORATE
MAGAZINE
DATE: 1987

1

2

3

4

1

Born in Rochdale, UK. Trained at Rochdale School of Art, Saint Martin's and the Royal College of Art. After graduating he taught at Cambridge School of Art and over the next ten years divided his time between teaching and freelance illustration for various publications, including the Radio Times, for whom he worked mostly in black and white. He also undertook private commissions and illustrated a letter-heading for the playwright Tom Stoppard, who owns several of his paintings. His early work in coloured pencils shows the influence of David Hockney, but his mature paintings are instantly recognizable as being in his own highly individual style. He illustrated several books, including Glynn Boyd Harte's Venice (1988), and exhibited at the Thumb and Francis Kyle galleries and the Albemarle Gallery in London.

1 "FOOD STILL LIFE"
DATE: NOT KNOWN

2 *PROMOTIONAL BROCHURE:* FONTANABOOKS
DATE: 1983

3 *SELF-PROMOTIONAL POSTER*
DATE: 1985

HOLIDAY READING

RECOMMENDED PAPERBACKS

2

GLYNN BOYD HARTE

THE REAL THING

3

ANDRZEJ DUDZINSKI
(b. 1945)

Born in Sopot, Poland. Initially studied architecture at Gdansk Polytechnic, but transferred after two years to the State College of Art, where he studied interior design and printmaking. He then studied poster design and painting at the Academy of Fine Art. He moved to New York in 1977, since then his work has appeared in various magazines and newspapers in Europe and the USA, including The Boston Globe, The New York Times, Newsweek, Playboy, Rolling Stone, Vogue, Vanity Fair, Time, Elle, Tatler *and* The Daily News. *He has exhibited at the National Arts Club in New York the Dubois Gallery in Pennsylvania, the Atrium in Connecticut and at the National Theatre in London. He taught at Parsons School of Design in New York and is currently visiting professor at the School of Visual Arts and New Media in Warsaw.*

1 *MAGAZINE:* THE DAILY NEWS
DATE: 1986

2 *POSTER:* SPECTATOR, XIII
DATE: 1983

3 *POSTER*
DATE: 1986

1

2

3

1

2

*Born in London. Studied at
Cambridge School of Art and
the Royal College of Art. Her
first illustrations were for* The
Sunday Times. *Since then she
has worked for Habitat stores,
Walker Books and a number
of advertising clients, and
contributed to* The Spectator
and A La Carte. *She has recently
designed a series of posters
for the Seibu department store
in Japan. She won the Lloyds
Printmakers Prize in 1981
and in 1985 her work was
represented in a British Council
exhibition entitled "From
Caxton to Chlöe".*

1 *MAGAZINE:* THE SUNDAY
TIMES
DATE: 1981

2 *BOOK:* SPECTATOR BOOK OF
TRAVEL WRITING
DATE: 1988

3 *MAGAZINE:* OBSERVER
DATE: 1985

3

1

2

3

4

Born in Texas, USA. Studied at
North Texas State University in
Denton, where he majored in
advertising art in 1968. After a
short period in an advertising
agency in Dallas, he was drafted
by the US Army and stationed in
Germany, where he developed
an interest in the fine arts. On
his return to the USA he studied
painting and drawing at East
Texas State University and
became a commercial artist
in 1972. After a brief spell
working as art director at the
University of Texas he became a
freelance illustrator. As well as
being commissioned by various
advertising agencies, his work
appeared in such publications
as Texas Monthly, Houston
City and D Magazine. In 1979
he co-founded the design and
illustration group Sagebrush
Studio and formed Curry and
Associates with two partners
in 1983.

1 *MAGAZINE:* ATLANTIC
MONTHLY
DATE: 1986

2 *MAGAZINE:* TEXAS MONTHLY
DATE: 1985

3 *MAGAZINE:* VIDEO
MAGAZINE
DATE: 1986

4 *ILLUSTRATION:* FOR
ADVANCED GRAPHIC SYSTEMS
CO.
DATE: 1987

CHRIS FOSS
(b. 1946)

Born in Devon, UK. As a child he loved to build models of steam engines and had a fascination for colour, speed and technology. While studying architecture at Cambridge University, he had a sci-fi comic strip published in Penthouse magazine. In 1970 one of his paintings appeared in Nova and this led to other commissions, most notably for Arthur C Clarke's Coming of the Space Age. *The following three years saw Foss establish himself as one of the most prolific and sought after science-fiction illustrators, with Isaac Asimov personally requesting that Foss should illustrate his* Foundation Series *(1973). Foss produces his highly detailed and colourful paintings in airbrush and his revolutionary view of technology and transport in the future has influenced the entire genre. He has also worked on three films, Richard Donner's* Superman *(1978) and Ridley Scott's* Alien *(1979) as well as Jodorowskis never-completed version of* Dune.

1 BOOK: WE CAN BUILD YOU
by Philip K Dick
DATE: 1986

2 BOOK: ASTEROID COLLISION
DATE: 1987

3 BOOK: STAR KING by Jack
Vance
DATE: 1988

1

2

3

*Born in O'Fallon, Illinois, USA.
Studied at the Washington
University School of Fine
Arts in St Louis, Missouri. He
began his career in 1957 in
Detroit, Michigan, working
on automobile accounts.
Later he moved to New York,
where he illustrated for The*
Saturday Evening Post, The New
Yorker *and* Sports Illustrated,
*among others. His exquisite
illustrations, which show
the influence of the French
Impressionists, ensured his
early success as both an
illustrator and a painter. At
the age of only 30 he was
named Artist of the Year by the
Artists Guild of New York and
in 1975 he was the youngest
artist ever to be elected to the
Illustrators Hall of Fame, since
then he has won the Hamilton
King Award and many gold
and silver medals from the
Society of Illustrators. He has
been commissioned to paint
the portraits of several U.S
presidents, including Kennedy
and Reagan. He has exhibited
his work in New York Chicago,
Atlanta, New Orleans, England,
Russia and Japan. In 1991 he
was named Sports Artist of the
Year by the American Sport, Art
and Museum Archives and has
also designed a series of postage
stamps on folk musicians.*

*1 RECORD ALBUM COVER:
TIME LIFE RECORDS
DATE.1980*

*2 POSTER: THE BIRTH
DEFECTS FOUNDATION
DATE.1988*

*3 MAGAZINE: TV GUIDE
DATE: NOT KNOWN*

ROBERT GROSSMAN
(b. 1940)

Born in New York. He was encouraged to draw as a child and attended Saturday morning art classes at the Museum of Modern Art in New York. He studied art at Yale, under Joseph Alber, and contributed illustrations to the college magazine, The Yale Record. *He also edited a magazine called* Yew Norker *– a spoof on* New Yorker *magazine – which, after he graduated in 1961, led to his first Job as a cartoon editor. Since becoming a freelance illustrator and cartoonist in 1965 he has illustrated for a number of magazines, including* Time, Newsweek, Esquire *and* Forbes. *He also designed the publicity poster for the film* Airplane, *taught at Syracuse University in New York and illustrated for a number of advertising clients.*

1 *MAGAZINE:* THE NEW REPUBLIC
DATE: 1988

2 *MAGAZINE:* FORBES
DATE: 1988

3 *MAGAZINE:* FORBES
DATE: 1988

4 *NEWSPAPER:* PENNSYLVANIA GAZETTE
DATE: 1988

1

2

3

4

BRIAN GRIMWOOD
(b. 1948)

1

2

3

Born in Beckenham, UK. Studied
at Bromley Technical High
School, where he was able to
study typography, life drawing
and graphics before the age of
16. He worked in an advertising
studio until he saw a Push Pin
Studios exhibition in 1968,
which inspired him to become
a freelance illustrator. Striving
to come up with "novel images
that will become classics", his
influences range from George
Grosz to Japanese packaging
and from Picasso to Seymour
Chwast, whom he met when he
visited New York in 1974. He
has worked for all the major
magazines and publications in
the UK, Europe and the USA and
for top advertising agencies all
over the world. He has exhibited
at all the Association of
Illustrators Annual Exhibitions
and the European Illustration
Annual Exhibitions since 1974
and has exhibited in London.
In 1983 he set up the Central
Illustration Agency, which now
represents 50 of the world's top
illustrators.

1 *GERMAN MAGAZINE:*
MANNERVOGUE
DATE: 1988

2 *BOOK.* QUIT SMOKING *by Dr
Miriam Stoppard*
DATE: 1981

3 *PERSONAL CHRISTMAS CARD*
DATE: 1988

1

2

3

4

5

*Born in New York. Attended the
High School of Music and Art,
then took evening classes at
the Art Students League. At the
Cooper Union Art School he won
a scholarship in 1952 to study
etching in Bologna, Italy, with
Giorgio Morandi. With Seymour
Chwast, Ed Sorel and Reynold
Ruffins, he co-founded the Push
Pin Studios in 1953 and* Push
Pin Graphic *in 1957, and in 1968
he founded* New York Magazine.
*He was also responsible for
the redesign of* Paris Match,
Cue, Village Voice, New West,
L'Express, L'Europeo, Jardin de
Modes *and* Esquire *magazines.
Books illustrated include* The
Milton Glaser Poster Book *(1977),
Asimov's* The Illustrated Don Juan
(1972), If Apples Had Teeth *(1960)
with Shirley Glaser and* Rimes de
la Mère Oie *(1971) with Seymour
Chwast and Barry Zaid. In 1974
he designed a huge mural for
the New Federal Office Building
New York, and in 1975 designed
the observation deck of the
twin towers of the World Trade
Centre. Glaser's distinctive work
influenced by Islamic and Indian
painting and Japanese woodcuts,
has won him many awards,
including a gold medal from the
Society of Illustrators.*

1 *POSTER*
DATE: 1986

2 *BOOK:* THE COLLECTED
WORKS OF APOLLINAIRE
DATE: 1983

3 *RECORD ALBUM COVER:*
ALBERT KING
DATE: 1976

4, 5 *END PAPER ILLUSTRATION
FOR BOOK ON GOGOL*
DATE: 1987

6 *PAINTING:* "SHIRLEY, ANNIE
AND MR HOFFMAN"
DATE: 1985

6

Born in New York. After graduating from the Art Students League and the Pratt Institute, he taught at a New York public school painting in his spare time. Recognizing that his paintings lent themselves well to magazine illustration, a friend took a selection of them to Esquire, and this led to his first commission. Since then his illustrations have appeared in most of the major American publications, including Village Voice, The New York Times, Esquire and Playboy. Citing the diverse influences of Robert Crumb, William Blake, Max Beckmann and René Magritte, he describes his work as a combination of surrealism and expressionism. Essentially a painter, he has exhibited in New York and Florida and has recently been working on "constructions" made with acrylic paints and cardboard.

1 MAGAZINE: VILLAGE VOICE
DATE: 1987

2. MAGAZINE: VILLAGE VOICE
DATE: 1989

3. MAGAZINE, VILLAGE VOICE
DATE: 1989

1

2

3

1   2   3

*Born in London. Studied at
the Central School of Art and
Crafts, where he was influenced
by his tutor, Bob Gill. After
graduating in 1973 he moved
to Los Angeles and set himself
up as a freelance illustrator.
He has worked prolifically ever
since and his brightly coloured,
intensely graphic illustrations
have appeared in all the
major American publications,
including* Time, The New Yorker,
Playboy, Esquire, Vanity Fair *and*
Rolling Stone. *He cites the soul
singer Otis Redding as a major
influence on his work and has
taught at the Art Centre in Los
Angeles and the Parsons School
of Design.*

1 *MAGAZINE:* CHIC
DATE: 1976

2 *MAGAZINE:* NEW YORK
MAGAZINE
DATE: 1975

3. *MAGAZINE:* LA STYLE
DATE: 1987

4 "MICKEY MONDRIAN"
(uncommissioned)
DATE: 1976

4

*Born in Cracow, Poland.
Educated at the Academies
of Fine Arts in Cracow and
Warsaw, graduating in 1976.
Since then she has held a
number of one-woman shows
in Poland, Paris, Italy, the
USA and Japan. Magazine*
clients include Playboy, Gallery,
Graphis, Elle *and* Penthouse
Letters *(USA),* Gunnars *and*
Mode Avantgarde *(France),* City
Life *(West Germany),* Asahigraph
and Illustration *(Japan) and*
Projekt, Szutka, ITD, Fantastyka
(Poland).

1 *MAGAZINE:* FANTASTYKA
DATE. 1988

2 *MAGAZINE:* CITY LIFE
DATE. 1988

1

2

Born in Marshalltown, Iowa, USA. Trained at Binding School of Art Sarasota, then went on to work as a staff artist for public television, as an assistant advertising director, a graphic designer and an editorial illustrator. Since 1978 she has concentrated on freelance illustration and her elegantly balanced compositions, subtle colours and great sense of action and movement have made her particularly popular with sports and news publications such as Golf, Sports Illustrated, World Report and US News. Her work has also appeared in books, including The Long March by Harrison Salisbury (1984), on record covers, posters and TV. She has won numerous awards, including the New York Society of Illustrators Award of Merit in 1984, the Award of Excellence, Communication Arts, New York, in 1985 and the 66th Art Directors Annual DESI Award. She has illustrated Vilma Martinez, a learning book for Spanish students.

1

1 *MAGAZINE:* SPORTS ILLUSTRATED
DATE. 1987

2 "SWAN" *(unpublished)*
DATE: c. 1987

3 "SHADE OF THE BEACH" *(unpublished)*
DATE: 1988

2

3

LIONEL KOECHLIN
(b. 1948)

Born in Paris. Trained at the Ecole Nationale Superieure des Métiers d'Art in the studio of general decoration, specializing in mural art, poster and theatre design for children. From the mid- 70s he has had work published in numerous magazines, including Marie Claire, Rock and Folk, La Recherche *and* Femme Pratique. *He has also illustrated a number of books, including his own* Le Rouge, Le Jaune *and* Le Bleu *(all 1984) and Jan Van Aal's depiction of the advertising industry in France,* Au Clair de la Pub *(1986). Advertising clients include KP, Hewlett Packard, Ward Air and Mobil Oil. His influences, which include the writings of Georges Simenon and the music of Louis Armstrong are broad and constantly changing as is the style and content of his work. He has had exhibitions in both Belgium and France.*

1 *BOOK:* ADVENTURES OF JOSEPH AND MIMI *by Anne-Marie Chapouton*
DATE: 1988

2 *LIMITED EDITION PRINT*
DATE: 1987

3 *MAGAZINE COVER:* THE NEW YORKER *(unpublished)*
DATE: 1982

4 *UNPUBLISHED*
DATE: 1979

5 *PUBLICITY POSTER*
DATE: 1987

1

2

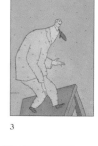

3

4

DESSINS

LIONEL KOECHLIN

L A R C
LE CREUSOT

5

1

2

THERE IS NO PEACE AFTER NUCLEAR WAR!

3

RAFAL OLBINSKI
(b. 1945)

*Born in Poland. He graduated
from the architectural
department of Warsaw
Polytechnical School with
a distinction in 1969, since
when he has achieved
international acclaim, his
illustrations appearing in*
Graphis *(Switzerland),* Novum
(Germany) and Idea *(Japan)
magazines, and in the American
publications* Time, Newsweek,
The New York Times *and*
Business Week. *He has also
illustrated for a number of
advertising clients. He cites his
influences as "everybody", from
Saul Steinberg to Milton Glaser,
Marshall Arisman and Brad
Holland, and characterizes his
work as "poetic surrealism". He
has won innumerable awards
for excellence in illustration
and design, including two silver
and one gold medal from the
Society of Illustrators, and is
represented at the Museum of
Modern Art (Poster Collection),
at the Carnegie Foundation in
New York, and at the Poster
Museum in Warsaw, Poland.
He lives in New York, where,
as well as being a freelance
illustrator, designer and painter,
he teaches at the School of
Visual Arts.*

1 *PUBLICITY POSTER:*
CARNEGIE HALL CONCERT
DATE: 1988

2 *POSTER:* "DOVE OF PEACE"
HIROSHIMA ANNIVERSARY
DATE: 1985

3 *BOOK JACKET:* THE FOOL
AND HIS MONEY
DATE: 1988

ROBERT PARKER
(b. 1927)

*Born in Norfolk, Virginia, USA.
Studied at the Art Institute of
Chicago and the Skowhegan
School of Painting and Sculpture
in Maine, where he was a
pupil of Jack Levine and Henry
Varnum Poor. His intention
was to be a fine artist and he
exhibited in 1952 at Atelier
17 in New York. Successful
one-man shows followed and
his work has been acquired
by the Museum of Modern Art,
the Metropolitan Museum of
Art and the Whitney Museum.
His career as an illustrator
began when a series of water
colours, painted for his son, was
published in* Esquire *magazine.
This inspired commissions
from several other magazines,
including the* Lamp, Playboy,
Sports Illustrated *and* Fortune,
*which sent him on several major
reportage assignments around
the world. He also worked in
the film industry, producing
the canvases for Kirk Douglass
portrayal of Van Gogh in* Lust for
Life, *and his water colours have
been used on film to illustrate
the poetry of Wilfred Owen and
Keith Douglas. He has taught
at the Pratt Institute, Parsons
School of Design and the Rhode
Island School of Design.*

1

2

---

1 "A DOUBLE PORTRAIT"
DATE: 1986

---

2 "A SCENE FROM GUNGA DIN"
DATE: 1987

---

3 "YOU STEPPED OUT OF A
DREAM"
DATE: 1987

3

1

2

Born in Cheshire, UK, and educated at Manchester Polytechnic and the Royal College of Art. As well as a number of one-man shows, he has exhibited in every European Illustration *Annual Exhibition and Association of Illustrators Annual Exhibition since 1975, and is represented in public collections throughout the UK, including the Victoria and Albert Museum and the Arts Council of Great Britain in London. He has illustrated for magazines such as* Rolling Stone *and* Men Only, *and designed the Lear poster for the National Theatre in London. He also does a large amount of design and advertising work, for clients such as Coopers and Lybrand BP and Saatchis. Books illustrated include* The Miracles of Christ *(1976),* Couples *(1979)* The Pepper Press Book of Catastrophes *(1981) and* Cartoon King Lear *(1984). He also designed* Tales of Terror *(1997), a series of postage stamps for the Royal Mail.*

1 *POSTER*
DATE: 1984

2 *MAGAZINE:* MEN ONLY
DATE. 1985

3 "DRUNK ON THE BOWERY"
DATE: 1987

4 *MAGAZINE:* ROLLING STONE
DATE. 1985

MARSHALL ARISMAN
(b. 1938)

Born in Jamestown, New York. On graduating in advertising art from the Pratt Institute in New York in 1960, he received the Ida Gaskill Grant to travel and study in Europe. After military service he worked as a graphic designer for General Motors, taking figure-drawing classes in the evenings. He then became an illustrator. He has had one-man shows in America, Europe and Japan and his paintings are in the permanent collections of the Brooklyn Museum and the National Museum of American Art. He has won awards from the Society of Illustrators, the American Institute of Graphic Arts, the Society of Publication Designers and American Illustration. Clients include The New York Times, The Nation, Mother Jones, Time and Penthouse magazines. Books illustrated include Fitcher's Bird (1983) and Frozen Images, a book of illustrations on the theme of violence. He also created The Last Tribe, a series of paintings, sculpture and video on the theme of the atomic bomb and the future of mankind. His influences include Andre François, Velázquez, Goya, primitive art and the British painter Francis Bacon, whose influence is particularly evident in violent and expressive images reflecting his concerns for the human condition.

1 MAGAZINE: THE NEW YORK TIMES
DATE: 1986

2 MAGAZINE: TIME
DATE: 1987

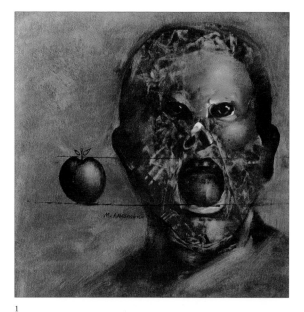

1

2

1

3 *ILLUSTRATION: (unpublished)*
DATE: 1987

4 *ILLUSTRATION: (unpublished)*
DATE: 1987

5 *MAGAZINE:* OMNI
DATE: 1986

6 *MAGAZINE:* OMNI
DATE: 1985

2

3

4

PAUL SAMPLE
(b. 1947)

Born in Leeds, UK. Studied at Bradford Art College and the Central School of Art in London. Since graduating in 1968 he has become well known for his humorous illustrations, particularly those for the Smirnoff Vodka and Listerine mouthwash advertising campaigns, and cites among his influences Dudley D Watkin, H M Bateman, Heath Robinson and George Morrow. He has illustrated for newspapers including the Daily Mirror, The Sunday Times *and* Observer, *and magazines, including* Penthouse, Management Today, Men Only, Bella *and* Campaign. *Additionally he has designed book jackets for the novels of Compton McKenzie, Tom Sharpe and Flann O'Brien, and did a monthly strip cartoon, "Ogri", for* Bike *magazine. He works mainly in pen and ink and watercolour wash.*

1 *ADVERTISEMENT:* SMIRNOFF VODKA
DATE: 1984

2 *MAGAZINE:* ARCHITECT'S JOURNAL
DATE: 1987

3 *BOOKJACKET:* THE THIRD POLICEMAN *by Flann O'Brien*
DATE: 1987

4 *BOOKJACKET:* VINTAGE STUFF *by Tom Sharpe*
DATE: 1983

1

2

3

4

Born in Indianapolis, Indiana, USA. Worked as an industrial designer and city planner for several years before studying illustration at Art Centre College, since then he has worked as an illustrator and painter. He has lived and worked in New York, Los Angeles and Chicago and carried out assignments for a number of book and magazine publishers and advertising clients. He has won a gold medal from The Society of Illustrators and awards from the Society of Publication Designers and the Chicago Artists' Guild.

1 *ILLUSTRATION FOR:* AMERICAN SOCIETY OF WOMEN ACCOUNTANTS *DATE:* 1989

2 *ILLUSTRATION FOR:* HUGHES UNITED PETROLEUM *DATE:* 1988

3 "STUDY OF AN ARM" *(unpublished)* *DATE:* 1987

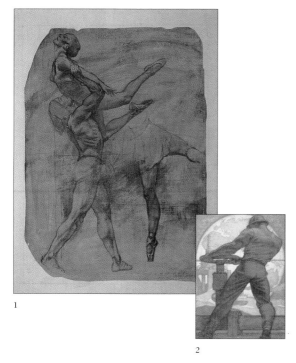

1

2

3

LANE SMITH
(b. 1959)

Born in California, USA. He graduated from the Art Centre College of Design in Pasadena, California, in 1983 and moved to New York the following year to take up freelance illustration. His work is regularly included in American Illustration *and he has won a silver medal from the* Society of Illustrators. *In 1987 his* Hallowe'en ABC *(written by Eve Merriam) was picked as one of the ten best books of the year by* The New York Times *and the best book of the year by the* School Library Journal. *He has also published a wordless picture book called* Flying Jake *(Macmillan, 1988). Magazine clients include* New York *and* Rolling Stone.

1 *MAGAZINE:* QUALITY
REVIEW
DATE: 1987

2 *BOOK:* HALLOWE'EN ABC *by Eve Merriam*
DATE: 1987

3 *MAGAZINE:* CAR STEREO
REVIEW
DATE: 1987

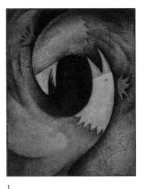

1

2

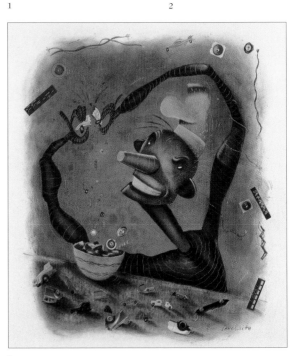

3

1

2

3

Born in Alpena, Michigan, USA. Trained at the Chicago Academy of Fine Arts (where he studied cartoon drawing) and at the Institute of Design in Chicago. He started his career in publishing then worked as an art director in advertising before turning to illustration. In 1976 he moved to New York, where his comic-book style of illustration featuring warm, whimsical and colourful characters was much in demand by greetings card companies, advertising clients and magazines such as Push Pin Graphic and New York. An admirer of his contemporaries Seymour Chwast and Milton Closer, as well as the cartoonists of old-time America – Rube Goldberg and George Herriman – he sees his style as a synthesis of old and new. He has won numerous awards for illustration and has written and illustrated two children's books, The See & Hear & Smell & Taste & Touch Book (1973) and A Ball of Yarns (1977). He lives in Rhinebeck, New York and illustrates for advertising clients and magazines.

1 *NEWSPAPER:* DALLAS TIMES
HERALD
DATE: 1986

2 *MAGAZINE:* MEDICAL SELF
CARE
DATE: 1988

3 *MAGAZINE:* TIME
DATE: 1987

Born in New York. Studied at the High School of Music and Art and Cooper Union School of Art, where he met Seymour Chwast and Milton Glaser (with whom he formed the Push Pin Studios in 1953). In 1957 he left Push Pin to concentrate on a career as a freelance illustrator, and drawn more and more to political satire, published his first cartoon book, How to be President, in 1960. Other books include Making the World Safe for Democracy (1972) and Moon Missing (1962). His regular contributions to Village Voice between 1974 and 1977 were eventually published as Superpen (1978). He has worked for a number of publications, including New York Magazine, Harper's, Esquire and The New York Times. In 1981 he won the George Polk Award for his satirical drawings, and in 1993 received the National Cartoonist Society Advertising and Illustration Award.

1

2

1 POSTER FOR: THE GRADUATE SCHOOL OF MANAGEMENT AND URBAN PROFESSIONS
DATE: 1986

2 MAGAZINE: GQ
DATE: 1988

3 MAGAZINE: ATLANTIC MONTHLY
DATE: 1986

4 BOOK JACKET: THINKING TUNA FISH, TALKING DEATH: ESSAYS ON THE PORNOGRAPHY OF POWER by Robert Scheer
DATE: 1988

5 MAGAZINE: AMERICAN HERITAGE
DATE: 1982

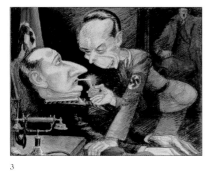

3

4

5

Born in Northumberland, UK. Trained at Newcastle upon Tyne College of Art and Hornsey College of Art, London. He joined Nicholas Thirkell Associates (a subdivision of Macmillan Publishing Ltd) in 1970 before forming NTA Studios with three partners in 1973. He has illustrated for publishing editorial, advertising and design groups in 13 countries. Publishing clients include Radio Times, Time Out, The Sunday Times, Design and Observer magazines. Advertising clients include Schweppes, Cadbury's, Knorr, the Greater London Council and the Milk Marketing Board. He has exhibited regularly in London, Paris, New York, Minneapolis and Amsterdam and won a number of awards, including a Design and Art Direction Annual silver in the UK and a Grammy Award nomination in the US. He enjoys composing images in which the elements are cohesive and yet retain a sense of rhythm and movement.

1 *BOOK:* THE CREATIVE
HANDBOOK DIARY
DATE: 1981

2 *CALENDAR DESIGN*
DATE: 1982

3 *MAGAZINE:* THE LISTENER
DATE: 1984

1

2

3

1

2

1

4

5

*Born in Horden, Co. Durham,
UK. Studied illustration at
Bristol and then taught art
part-time at a south London
comprehensive school. In 1973,
after he decided to abandon
teaching and become a freelance
illustrator, he presented a
commissioned drawing to
New Society magazine, only
to be told that their letterpress
printer couldn't reproduce
his delicate half-tones. It was
this disappointment that
led him to experiment with
scraperboard, a technique that
he uses exclusively today. He
has worked for many of the
major publications in London,
including The Times, Time
Out, Radio Times, New Society
and the New Scientist, and in
America contributes regularly
to Esquire, illustrating such
diverse subjects as outdoor
pursuits, personality profiles,
the gossip columns and the
sports clinic. He has advertising
clients both in the UK and USA
and illustrated Harry Harrison's
West of Eden trilogy in 1988. As
might be expected of an artist
working on scraperboard, his
influences are predominantly
19th century and he cites
Cruickshank and Doré as
particular inspirations.*

1 *MAGAZINE:* NEW SCIENTIST
DATE: 1987

2 *MAGAZINE:* NEW SCIENTIST
DATE: 1988

3 *MAGAZINE:* NEW SCIENTIST
DATE: 1986

4 *CATALOGUE:* WINE SOCIETY
DATE: 1987

5 *MAGAZINE:* ESQUIRE
DATE: 1988

HELEN OXENBURY
(b. 1938)

Born in Ipswich, UK. Studied at Ipswich School of Art and the Central School of Art in London, specializing in theatre design. After graduating she worked in theatre, film and television. She began illustrating children's books when expecting her first child. In 1967 The Number of Things *was published and immediately established her as a major picture book artist. In 1970 she won the Kate Greenaway Medal for her illustrations for Lear's* Quangle Wangle's Hat *and* The Dragon of an Ordinary Family. Since then her simple and observant watercolours have illustrated many internationally acclaimed children's books, including the First Picture Books (1983) and the Pippo series.

1 BOOK: DANCING CLASS by Helen Oxenbury
DATE: 1983

2 BOOK: THE CHECK-UP by Helen Oxenbury
DATE: 1983

3 BOOK: TICKLE TICKLE by Helen Oxenbury
DATE: 1987

4 BOOK: WE'RE GOING ON A BEAR HUNT by Helen Oxenbury and Michael Rosen
DATE: 1989

1

2

3

Stumble trip!
Stumble trip!
Stumble trip!

4

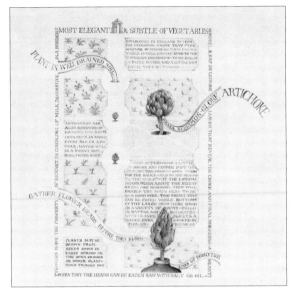

1

2

3

*Born in Brighton, UK. Trained
at Goldsmith's and Saint
Martin's. Midda is much
admired for her very fine,
delicate and beautifully coloured
illustrations, and the wonderful
sense of humour which is
evident in all her work. Her
first book,* In and Out of the
Garden *(1982), in which the
hand lettering is an integral
part of the image, won her the
Francis Williams V&A National
Book League Award for Best
Descriptive Illustration in
1982. She has also illustrated
for* Harpers & Queen, The
Sunday Times *and* Cosmopolitan
magazines and The Guardian
and The New York Times
*newspapers. She also designs
a line of products (from food
packaging and baby-wear to
bed-linen and china) under her
own name for the Mitsukoshi
department store in Japan. She
has exhibited at the Cartoon,
Langton, Thumb and Chris
Beetles Galleries in London.*

1, 3 *BOOK:* IN AND OUT OF
THE GARDEN *by Sara Midda*
DATE: 1982

2 *CHRISTMAS CARD*
DATE: 1984

DAN FERN
(b. 1945)

Born in Eastbourne, UK. Studied graphics at Manchester College of Art and illustration at the Royal College of Art in London. As well as various advertising agencies he has illustrated for The Sunday Times, Radio Times, New Scientist and Design magazines, Penguin, Pan and Time-Life books, Arista, Chrysalis and A&M records, Conran Design, Pentagram, Thames Television, the Royal Court Theatre, the BBC and the Joint Stock Theatre Group. He was a member of the jury of the Francis Williams Award for Book Illustration in 1982 and has himself won both gold and silver D&AD awards. He is a regular juror on the D&AD Annual for whom he also runs workshops. He became Head of Illustration at the Royal College of Art in 1986, and was appointed the first Professor of Illustration at the Royal College in 1989. Fern is a designer as well as an illustrator, and his interest in stamps and printed ephemera is reflected in the letter and number forms which are often incorporated into his work. He works mainly with paper and collage, and also has an interest in computer-generated design and illustration.

1

1 WINNER'S CERTIFICATE: BBC DESIGN AWARDS
DATE: 1987

2 POSTER: LONDON REGIONAL TRANSPORT
DATE: 1988

3 COVER: ART DIRECTORS CLUB OF HOLLAND ANNUAL
DATE: 1986

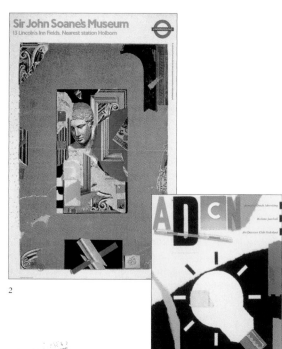

2

3

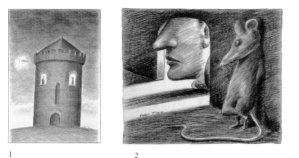

1   2

3

Born in Manchester, UK. He studied English Literature at Cambridge University and after graduating in 1967 worked mainly in theatre, doing illustrations as a sideline. In the early 70s he became a full-time illustrator, since when he has won a number of design and illustration awards. He has worked in advertising in Britain, Germany, Holland, the US, Sweden, Denmark and Singapore. Magazine clients include The Sunday Times, Observer, New York, Esquire, Gentlemen's Quarterly *and* Vogue. *In 1978 he made an animated film,* The Beard. *Citing Saul Steinberg as among his influences, he is entirely self-taught as an artist. His images have an element of the surreal and he enjoys juxtaposing disparate elements as a way of inviting viewers to make their own interpretations of the work.*

1 *POSTER:* ABERYSTWYTH
ARTS CENTRE
DATE: 1988

2 *MAGAZINE COVER:* THE
LISTENER
DATE: 1987

3 *MAGAZINE COVER:* NEW
SCIENTIST
DATE: 1987

JIM BURNS
(b. 1948)

Born in Cardiff, Wales. In 1966
he joined the Royal Air Force as
a trainee pilot but left in 1968
to study at Newport School
of Art, then at Saint Martin's
School of Art in London, from
where he received a diploma
in art and design. He has
painted numerous book and
paperback covers, for Sphere,
Corgi Tandem, Quartet, Coronet,
Methuen and Fontana Books.
In 1980 he assisted Ridley Scott
on designs for the film Blade
Runner. He has also illustrated
a series of novels by Robert
Silverberg for Bantam Books
and a collection of short stories
entitled Eye (1985) by Frank
Herbert. Burns specializes
in historical romances and
science fiction; in gouache,
acrylic, watercolour and oil. A
collection of his work featuring
one hundred colour illustrations
was published by Dragon's
World in 1986. His work has
recently been fetching a high
price at Sothebys and the major
Washington gallery, Worlds of
Wonder.

1 BOOK: OTHER EDENS
DATE: 1987

2 BOOK: THE CONGLOMEROID
COCKTAIL PARTY by Robert
Silverberg
DATE: 1985

3 BOOK: THE CHANTRY GUILD
by Gordon R Dickson
DATE: 1988

4 FRONTIER CROSSINGS"
DATE: 1987

5 BOOK: FREEWAY FIGHTER by
Ian Livingstone
DATE: 1984

1

2

3

4

5

1

2

3

RALPH STEADMAN
(b. 1936)

4

5

6

7

8

Born in Cheshire, UK. Studied part-time at the London College of Printing and took the Percy V Bradshaw Press Arts School course. He drew political cartoons for Private Eye *when it first appeared in 1961 and at about the same time, discovered George Grosz and John Heartfield whose powerful and caustic statements against the Establishment were a stimulus to his own work. The author Hunter S Thompson was another major influence. Their collaboration culminated in Steadman being voted Illustrator of the Year by the American Institute of Graphic Arts in 1979. His extraordinary range has ensured him equal acclaim for his children's illustrations, and his version of* Alice in Wonderland *(1967) won the Francis Williams Book Illustration Award in 1973. Steadman has worked on advertising campaigns and currently illustrates Will Self's column in* The Independent *newspaper.*

4 *MAGAZINE:* SATURDAY NIGHT
DATE: 1978

5 *COLLAGE/ MIXED MEDIA:* "FALKLANDS WAR"
DATE: 1982

6 *MAGAZINE:* ROLLING STONE
DATE: 1980

7 *MAGAZINE:* PENTHOUSE
DATE: 1979

8 *BOOK:* ALICE IN WONDERLAND *by Lewis Carroll*
DATE: 1967

*Born in London. Studied at
Wimbledon School of Art and
the Slade School. He has written
and illustrated several children's
books and in 1964 his* Fee Fi
Fo Fum *was runner-up for the
Kate Greenaway Medal, an
award he won in 1966 with the
publication of* The Mother Goose
Treasury, *and again in 1973
with* Father Christmas. *He works
in a variety of media – pencil,
crayons, gouache, watercolour
and line – to produce richly
colourful drawings which are
often presented in the format
of a strip cartoon. Two of his
books have been made into
films:* The Snowman *(1978), the
wistful story of a child's dream
told entirely in pictures, was
adapted by Briggs for television
in 1982 and* When the Wind
Blows *(1982), a despairing adult
story of life after the nuclear
holocaust, was made into a
full-length animated feature. He
continued to produce work for
children, with the* Unlucky Wally
series and The Bear, *and his
graphic novel* Ethel and Ernest
*won Best Illustrated Book in the
1998 British Book Awards.*

1 *BOOK:* THE SNOWMAN *by
Raymond Briggs*
DATE: 1978

2 *BOOK:* FATHER CHRISTMAS
by Raymond Briggs
DATE: 1973

1

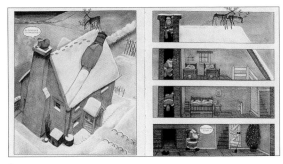

2

1

2

Born in London. After leaving school he worked for his uncle, a commercial artist, took evening classes in figure drawing at Saint Martin's School of Art and attended drawing classes at the Victoria & Albert Museum. In 1960 he started drawing for Punch, The Evening Standard *and* The Daily Sketch *and in 1964 was sent by* The Sunday Times *magazine to cover the Goldwater-Johnson elections in the USA. He worked there intermittently for two years, producing several covers for* Time *magazine and working as a reportage artist. In 1966 he undertook similar projects for the* Daily Mail *and* The Sunday Times *in London. His cartoons use an exquisite sense of line to cruelly caricature political and public figures, but his satirical eye has not confined its vision to the printed page. He has had an exhibition of his papier-mâché models at the National Portrait Gallery, has designed for the theatre and opera and made animated films for the BBC and Alan Parker's feature* Pink Floyd: The Wall. *In recent years he has directed award-winning documentaries for television and comedies for Channel 4. In 2006 he was awarded Cartoonist of the Year at the British Press Awards.*

1-2 *PUBLICITY POSTER:* PINK FLOYD: THE WALL
DATE: 1980

3 *COSTUME DESIGN:* ORPHEUS IN THE UNDERWORLD
DATE: 1983

3

PIERRE LE TAN
(b. 1950)

Born in Paris. Studied briefly at L'Ecole des Arts Decoratifs in Paris before pursuing a career as a freelance illustrator. By the age of 18 he had already sold two covers to The New Yorker *magazine, and over the next few years his work appeared predominantly in such American publications as* The New York Times, Harper's Bazaar *and* Atlantic. *He illustrated the books of American author John Train and in 1977 started to write and illustrate children's stories, including* The Afternoon Cat *(19 77) and* A Trip to the North Pole *(1988). The striking simplicity of his style has proved popular with advertising agencies and he has illustrated campaigns for Glenfiddich whisky in America, Manpower Services in the UK and Gallery Lafayette in Paris. Although he professes no great love of travelling he has a column in Condé Nast's* The Traveller, *in which he visits and illustrates various locations around the world. He still lives and works in Paris, where he is taking fewer commissions and concentrating on his own adult writing. He wrote and illustrated* Rencontres d'une Vie *in 1986 and* Paris de ma jeunesse *in 1988.*

1

2

3

4

1 *MAGAZINE:* THE NEW
YORKER
DATE: 1987

2 *MAGAZINE:* THE NEW
YORKER
DATE: 1980

3 *BOOK:* RENCONTRES D'UNE
VIE
by Pierre Le Tan
DATE: 1986

4 *EXHIBITION INVITATION*
DATE: 1980

1

2

3

4

*Born in London. While still
at school he won a National
Portrait Gallery competition,
and his entry was a London
Underground poster publicizing
the gallery. He studied at
Chelsea School of Art under
Susan Einzig, whom he cites
as a major influence and
who introduced him to the
illustrators of the 40s and 50s,
"the golden age of illustration".
While still a student he received
his first major commission,
designing greetings cards for
Jan Pienkowski's company
Gallery Five in 1973. While
studying at the Royal College
of Art he illustrated for a
number of publishers and
magazines, including* Tatler
and Vogue *(where he has been
a contributing editor on the
permanent staff since 1989).
He has taught at Hornsey,
Wolverhampton and Berkshire
Art Colleges, and wrote a
regular column, "Modern
Types", for the* Observer
*newspaper throughout 1987.
Describing himself as "a
commercial artist rather
than an illustrator", he has
designed costumes and sets
for video and theatre, and also
paints portraits and murals.
He illustrates in a range of
styles, making a speciality of
affectionate pastiche.*

1 *BOOK:* COTTON COMES TO
HARLEM *by Chester Himes*
DATE: 1984

2 *MAGAZINE:* THE SPECTATOR
DATE: 1982

3 *MAGAZINE:* TATLER
DATE: 1982

4 *BOOK:* LORD BYRON:
SELECTED LETTERS AND
JOURNALS
DATE: 1984

Born in Suffolk, UK. Trained at the Royal College of Art, where he won a scholarship to the USA in 1963. He was art director on Playboy, King *and* Ambit *magazines and has made animated films in Scandinavia and for the BBC in the UK. He has written and illustrated 14 books for children, including* War and Peas *(1974),* Panda and his Voyage of Discovery *(1977),* Panda and the Odd Lion *(1979) and* War Boy *(1989), and also illustrated* The Saga of Erik the Viking *(1983) and* Nicobobinus *(1986) by Terry Jones,* Tales for the Telling *(1986) by Edna O'Brien and Rudyard Kipling's* Just So stories *(1987). His expressive and sensitive watercolour illustrations have won him several awards, including the Silver Eagle prize at the Festival International du Livre, France (1972), first prize in the Francis Williams Book Illustrations Award (1972 and 1977), the Graphics Prize at Bologna (1982) and the Kurt Maschler Award (1982). He won the Nestle Smarties Book Prize in 1993 for* After the War Was Over *which he wrote and illustrated.*

1-2 *BOOK:* THE SAGA OF ERIK THE VIKING *by Terry Jones*
DATE: 1983

3 *BOOK:* WAR BOY: A SUFFOLK CHILDHOOD *by Michael Foreman*
DATE: 1989

1

2

3

1

2

3

4

5

6

Born in Kendal, UK. Studied at Manchester College of Art and Saint Martin's. From 1946-48 he was a staff illustrator for Shell, after which he began his life as artist-traveller. Hogarth was prolific during the 50s, illustrating Jane Eyre *(1954),* The Adventures of Sherlock Holmes *(1958),* The Gold of the Snow Goose *(1958) and* King Solomon's Mines *(1958) as well as writing and illustrating* Looking at China *(1956) and* People Like Us *(1958). During the 60s he made a name for himself on the pages of* Fortune *and* Sports Illustrated *and also collaborated with Brendan Behan on books about Ireland and New York. His illustrations for Robert Graves'* Poems *gained him a Francis Williams Illustration Award for best illustration in 1983. His best-known works are those based on his own extensive travels, and his classic survey,* Artist as Reporter, *received the Yorkshire Post Award as the best art book of 1986. He illustrated many covers for Penguin Books, including all of Graham Greene's novels since 1962, and provided illustrations for John Betjeman's* In Praise of Churches *(1996).*

1 *BOOK:* WALKING TOURS OF OLD WASHINGTON AND ALEXANDRIA *by Paul Hogarth*
DATE: 1985

2- 4 *BOOK:* GRAHAM GREENE COUNTRY *by Paul Hogarth*
DATE: 1986

5 *BOOK:* NEW PENGUIN SHAKESPEARE: TROILUS AND CRESSIDA
DATE: 1989

6 *BOOK:* NEW PENGUIN SHAKESPEARE: VENUS AND ADONIS
DATE: 1989

Born in *New York. Studied
graphic design at the Cooper
Union School in New York,
where he met Milton Glaser,
Reynold Puffins and Ed Sorel
with whom he co-founded the
celebrated Push Pin Studios
in 1953. After graduating
he worked for* The New York
Times *and* Esquire, House
and Garden *and* The Boston
Globe *magazines. In 1953 he
privately published* A Book of
Battles, *and in 1985 produced
his own retrospective volume,*
Seymour Chwast: The Left
Handed Designer. *In 1982 he and
Alan Peckolick formed Pushpin
Lubalin Peckolick. Clients have
included leading corporations,
advertising agencies and
publishing companies in the
USA and abroad. He has won
numerous design awards,
including the St Gauden's
medal from Cooper Union, and
was elected to the Art Directors
Club Hall of Fame. He cites Ben
Shahn as a major influence on
his work and the immediacy
and directness of his style
has become synonymous with
the "Push Pin style", which
has had enormous influence
internationally.*

1,4 *BOOK:* HAPPY BIRTHDAY
BACH *by Seymour Chwast &
Peter Schickele*
DATE: 1986

2 *BOOK:* SAM'S BAR *edited by
Steven Heiter*
DATE: 1987

3 *THEATRE POSTER*
DATE: 1986

5 *POSTER:* FORBES MAGAZINE
DATE. 1967

1

2

3

1

2

BRAD HOLLAND
(b. 1943)

1

2

3

1

2

Born in Fremont, Ohio, USA. At 17 he left home and moved to Chicago, where he worked for a short time as a tattoo artist, then as a "short-order" artist. In Kansas City in 1964 he formed Asylum Press to print "eccentric projects with friends". In 1967 Holland moved to New York City, and contributed to various underground magazines. In 1971 he became one of the founding artists of the Op-Ed page of The New York Times. He also designed postage stamps for the US government, executed a mural for the United Nations Building in New York, contributed to Playboy, Time and Newsweek, and wrote a book Human Scandals (1977). As well as displaying an exquisite technique with both pen and brush Holland's illustrations invariably contain powerful images, often achieved with the incongruous yet revealing juxtaposition of symbols. His work has won gold medals from the Art Directors' Club of New York the Society of Illustrators and the Society of Publication Designers.

1 "DETAILS AT ELEVEN"
(unpublished)
DATE: 1987

2 MAGAZINE: FRANKFURTER
ALLGEMEINE "MICKEY MOUSE
ON SIXTH AVENUE"
DATE: 1987

3 MAGAZINE: FRANKFURTER
ALLGEMEINE "THE DINOSAUR
LOUNGE"
DATE: 1988

4 MAGAZINE: FRANKFURTER
ALLGEMEINE "BLUE
POOLROOM"
DATE: 1988

5 MAGAZINE: FRANKFURTER
ALLGEMEINE "THREE
GREYHOUNDS"
DATE: 1987

CREDITS

RICHARD ADAMS: **262, 263**; AMNESTY INTERNATIONAL: **250**; BERNARD D'ANDREA: **254**; MARSHALL ARISMAN: **288, 289**; AUTHOR'S COLLECTION: **40, 72, 73, 82, 89, 221**; GUY BILLOUT: **268**; PETER BLAKE: **214**; QUENTIN BLAKE: **246, 247**; BODLEY HEAD: **253**; GLYN BOYD HARTE: **269**; BRIDGEMAN ART LIBRARY: **24, 27, 48, 49, 51, 112**; MICK BROWNFIELD: **265**; JIM BURNS: **302, 303**; DAVE CALVER: **264**; JONATHAN CAPE: **220, 224, 245, 256, 257**; PHILIP CASTLE: **267**; JEAN LOUP CHARMET: **44, 45, 48,50, 128, 143, 251**; CHLOE CHEESE: **271**; CHRISTIES COLOUR LIBRARY: **141** SEYMOUR CHWAST: **312, 313**; COUNTRY LIFE: **213**; TOM CURRY: **272** DAILY EXPRESS: **212** ROGER DEAN MAGNETIC STORM: **242, 243**; ANDRE DUDZINSKI: **270**; EMI: **214**; ESTATE OF M.C. ESCHER (CORDON ART BV): **170**; E T ARCHIVE: **15, 19, 23, 26, 27, 30, 31, 32, 33, 36, 38, 41, 42, 45, 46, 48, 66, 74, 76, 81, 82, 83, 87, 90, 91, 100, 113, 117, 119, 134, 135, 146, 148, 161, 168, 192, 194, 201, 203, 224, 236**; FABER AND FABER **224, 236**; FANTAGRAPHIC BOOKS: **223**; FELMINGHAM COLLECTION: **27, 37, 41, 65, 74, 107, 117, 144, 145, 205, 218, 222, 224, 227**; DAN FERN: **300**; FOLON: **215**; MICHAEL FOREMAN: **310**; CHRIS FOSS: **274**; BERNIE FUCHS: **275**; DAVID GENTLEMAN, PENGUIN: **247**; MILTON GLASER: **278-279**; BRIAN GRIMWOOD: **277**; ROBERT GROSSMAN: **276**; GUINNESS: **225**; WALTER GURBO: **280**; MICK HAGGERTY: **281-2**; HAMISH HAMILTON: **306**; HARRAP; **159**; WILLIAM HEINEMANN: **252**; PAUL HOGARTH: **311**; JOHN HODGSON ILLUSTRATOR'S AGENCY, LONDON: **284-5**; BRAD HOLLAND: **314-5**; ICA: **251**; PETER JACKSON COLLECTION: **96, 178, 187, 204, 237**; PETER ANDREW JONES. COPYRIGHT: SOLAR WIND LIBRARY: **249**; MARZENA KAWALEROWICZ: **282**; SUSAN KILGORE: **283**; DAVID KING COLLECTION: **165, 166, 167, 172, 173**; ROGER LAW: **233**; PAUL LEITH, SHARP PRACTICE: **258**; LIBRARY OF CONGRESS: **228**; LONDON TRANSPORT MUSEUM: **120, 126, 140, 152, 156, 161, 163, 168, 169, 220**; BRIAN LOVE: **230-1**; MASTERS OF COMIC BOOK ART. AURUM PRESS: **229**; MEPL: **16, 17, 25, 30, 31, 34, 51, 42, 47, 49, 51, 52, 64, 67, 77, 86, 89, 96, 98, 99, 101, 103, 105, 106, 109, 111, 112, 113, 116, 126, 127, 131, 137, 141, 146, 147, 152, 168**; MEPL/MRS HILARY WICKHAM: **118, 119**; METHUEN: **7, 147, 157, 158, 199**; SARA MIDDA: **299**; JACQUI MORGAN: **255**; MUSEE DE LA PUBLICITE PARIS: **54, 75**; MUSEUM FUR GESTALTUNG. ZURICH: **80, 88, 95, 114, 115, 121, 129, 154, 157, 160, 182, 188, 193, 196, 201, 211, 215**; LAURENCE MYNOTT: **309**; BILL NELSON: **262**; BARBARA NESSIM: **259**; NEWMAN COLLECTION: **122, 123, 125, 133**; NIXDORF COMPUTER: **253**; RAFAL OLBINSKI: **285**; ROBERT OPIE COLLECTION: **38, 61, 112, 118, 133, 136, 151, 152, 171, 183, 195**; III **183, 186, 217**; ROBERT PARKER: **286**; MERVYN PEAKE ESTATE: **184-5**; PEN GUIN: **158**; BRUCE PENNINGTON AND DRAGONS WORLD: **248**; IAN POLLOCK: **287**; POLYGON EDITIONS: **180**; PUNCH: **181, 183, 187**; RANDOM HOUSE: **216**; RETROGRAPH ARCHIVE COLLECTION: **39, 44, 60, 81, 110, 114, 130, 153, 155, 157, 189, 201**; THE ESTATE OF WILLIAM HEATH ROBINSON (LAURENCE POLL) **164**; ROUNDABOUT THEATRE NEW YORK: **251**; JOHN RUSH: **291**; PAUL SAMPLE: **290**; REPRODUCED BY KIND PERMISSION OF SHELL UK LTD: **108, 132, 136, 151, 153, 156, 169**; LANE SMITH **292**; LINE ILLUSTRATIONS BY EH. SHEPARD COPYRIGHT UNDER BERNE CONVENTION AND IN THE UNITED STATES COPYRIGHT **1933** CHARLES SCRIBNERS SONS. RENEWAL COPYRIGHT © **1961** ERNEST H SHEPARD ERNEST H SHEPARD REPRODUCED BY PERMISSION OF CURTIS BROWN, LONDON: **158**; RALPH STEADMAN, SATURDAY NIGHT MAGAZINE: **305**; RALPH STEADMAN, ROLLING STONE MAGAZINE: **305**; RALPH STEADMAN, PENTHOUSE MAGAZINE: **305**; RALPH STEADMAN, ALICE IN WONDERLAND: **305**; RALPH STEADMAN, SATURDAY NIGHT MAGAZINE: **304**; RALPH STEADMAN, STAR STRANGLED BANNER: **304**; RENEE STREET: **260**; RUFUS PUBLICATIONS: **200**; SATURDAY EVENING POST/FELMINGHAM COLLECTION: **226**; GERALD SCARFE: **307**; SHELL UK LTD: **161**; ELWOOD SMITH: **293**; COLLECTION OF SOCIETY OF ILLUSTRATORS MUSEUM OF AMERICAN ILLUSTRATION: **65, 179, 207, 209, 221, 226, 235**; EDWARD SOREL: **294-5**; SPITTING IMAGE PRODUCTIONS LTD: **266**; GEOFF STEAR COLLECTION: **124**; DAVID STREET: **261**; SUNDAY TIMES/FELMINGHAM COLLECTION: **232**; SUNDAY TIMES/DAVID KING COLLECTION: **233**; PIERRE LE TAN. NEW YORKER: **308**; PIERRE LE TAN: **308**; PETER TILL: **301**; THORNTON UTZ: **208**; V AND A/PHOTO EILEEN TWEEDY: **39, 43, 75, 79, 85, 86, 87, 97, 100, 108, 120, 127, 133, 136, 138, 139, 149, 150, 158, 160, 182, 197, 198, 203, 206, 210, 220**; VOGUE: **211**; WALKER BOOKS: **298**; WARD LOCK: **71**; © FREDERICK WARNE & CO., 1903, 1987: **62**; © FREDERICK WARNE & CO., 1902, 1987: **62**; © FREDERICK WARNE & CO., 1907, 1987; © FREDERICK WARNE & CO., 1907; © FREDERICK WARNE & CO., 1904, 1987; PETER NEWARK'S WESTERN AMERICANA: **68, 77, 94, 102, 107, 127**; WOMAN/AUTHOR'S COLLECTION: **234**

EVERY EFFORT HAS BEEN MADE TO TRACE AND ACKNOWLEDGE ALL COPYRIGHT HOLDERS, QUARTO WOULD LIKE TO APOLOGIZE IF ANY OMISSIONS HAVE BEEN MADE.

THIS BOOK CONTAINS EXAMPLES OF GRAPHIC DESIGN WORK. THESE EXAMPLES ARE INCLUDED FOR THE PURPOSE OF CRITICISM AND REVIEW.